T0329381

CAMBRIDGE LIBRARY COLLECTION

Books of enduring scholarly value

History

The books reissued in this series include accounts of historical events and movements by eye-witnesses and contemporaries, as well as landmark studies that assembled significant source materials or developed new historiographical methods. The series includes work in social, political and military history on a wide range of periods and regions, giving modern scholars ready access to influential publications of the past.

Every Man his Own Broker

Thomas Mortimer (1730–1810) is chiefly remembered as a writer on economics. *Every Man His Own Broker* was first published in 1761, and ran to fourteen editions in the next forty years, this reissue being of the fourth edition. It was based on his own experience of the stock market, which in the first half of the eighteenth century was rapidly developing, but also suffered crises in which many speculators lost heavily. Increasing sales of government stock to pay for foreign wars led to concern, and Mortimer gives practical advice enabling readers to avoid making mistakes by relying on brokers. The book gives a good picture of how the stock market and the London financial world were operating at this time, although Mortimer's antipathy to brokers and jobbers is exaggerated. The book contains the first use of the terms 'bull' and 'bear' to describe types of markets.

Cambridge University Press has long been a pioneer in the reissuing of out-of-print titles from its own backlist, producing digital reprints of books that are still sought after by scholars and students but could not be reprinted economically using traditional technology. The Cambridge Library Collection extends this activity to a wider range of books which are still of importance to researchers and professionals, either for the source material they contain, or as landmarks in the history of their academic discipline.

Drawing from the world-renowned collections in the Cambridge University Library, and guided by the advice of experts in each subject area, Cambridge University Press is using state-of-the-art scanning machines in its own Printing House to capture the content of each book selected for inclusion. The files are processed to give a consistently clear, crisp image, and the books finished to the high quality standard for which the Press is recognised around the world. The latest print-on-demand technology ensures that the books will remain available indefinitely, and that orders for single or multiple copies can quickly be supplied.

The Cambridge Library Collection will bring back to life books of enduring scholarly value (including out-of-copyright works originally issued by other publishers) across a wide range of disciplines in the humanities and social sciences and in science and technology.

Every Man
his Own Broker

Or, A Guide to Exchange-Alley

THOMAS MORTIMER

CAMBRIDGE
UNIVERSITY PRESS

CAMBRIDGE UNIVERSITY PRESS

Cambridge, New York, Melbourne, Madrid, Cape Town, Singapore,
São Paolo, Delhi, Dubai, Tokyo, Mexico City

Published in the United States of America by Cambridge University Press, New York

www.cambridge.org
Information on this title: www.cambridge.org/9781108025829

© in this compilation Cambridge University Press 2010

This edition first published 1761
This digitally printed version 2010

ISBN 978-1-108-02582-9 Paperback

EVERY MAN
HIS OWN
BROKER:
OR,
A GUIDE to EXCHANGE-ALLEY.

IN WHICH
The Nature of the feveral FUNDS, vulgarly called the
STOCKS, is clearly explained.

AND
The Myftery and Iniquity of STOCK-JOBBING laid before
the Public in a New and Impartial Light.

ALSO
The Method of Transferring STOCK, and of Buying and Selling
the feveral GOVERNMENT SECURITIES, without the Affiftance of a BROKER, is made intelligible to the meaneft Capacity : and an Account is given of the Laws in force relative to
BROKERS, Clerks at the Bank, &c.

To which is added,
New TABLES of INTEREST on INDIA BONDS, calculated at 5 *per
Cent.*—Directions how to avoid the Loffes that are frequently fuftained
by the Deftruction of BANK NOTES, INDIA BONDS, &c. by Fires
and other Accidents. And an APPENDIX, giving fome Account of
Banking, and of the Sinking Fund.—With a Copper-Plate TABLE,
fhewing the intrinfic Value of the feveral Funds, and the Proportion
they bear to each other, by which any Perfon may immediately know
which is the cheapeft to purchafe.

Quid faciunt leges, ubi fola pecunia regnat.

THE FOURTH EDITION,

By T. MORTIMER.

LONDON:
Printed for S. HOOPER, at Cæfar's Head, the Corner of the
New Church in the Strand. M.DCC.LXI.

PREFACE.

SUM SOLUS, I remember, was the motto of a very singular man, after whom the good people of England ran in crowds some few years ago, according to their usual curiosity, and taste for novelty. His excellence consisted in broiling a beef-steak upon his tongue, and eating an infernal soop, composed of various combustibles, without burning his mouth. After this account of him, the sagacious reader will be apt to think, no man has a better title than this, to the motto at the head of the page. Certain it is, however, that my pretensions to it go much further than his, as I never heard that he favoured the public with a trea-

tise

tife upon his excellent art—no, to me
alone it was referved to teach aftonifhed
Britons, the amazing art of thrufting their
hands into the fire * without burning
their fingers ; or, in other words, of
teaching grown people to walk thro' the
fiery furnace of J————'s Coffee-houfe
unhurt ; a tafk extremely difficult for
a Chriftian author to perform, and equally hard for a Chriftian people to attain.
Shadrach, Mefhach, and Abednego,
have indeed granted policies of infurance to all their defcendents, and therefore it is rare to fee a Jew fo much as
finge his beard, in this manfion of Belze-
bub ; while poor Chriftians very often
confume bills, bonds, and jewels, in a
few days, betwixt the hours of one and
three, when its heat is moft intenfe. Ar-
duous as the tafk is, I hope, however,
to acquit myfelf with honour, and to the

---

* A phrafe well known to the gentlemen of
'Change-Alley.

no

no fmall profit and entertainment of my readers.

I am aware, that prefaces are generally turned over as ufelefs lumber, by moft readers; I therefore am obliged, in this place, to caution mine, againft this common error, as it will be extremely necef-fary for the right underftanding the following pages, to read this Preface with attention, in which feveral curious and interefting circumftances are laid open, which could not, with any propriety, be thrown into the body of this little piece. The author is thoroughly fenfible, that his undertaking will create him a levy of enemies; for when it is confider-ed what numbers live by the iniquity which he intends to difclofe, and in fome meafure to defeat the effect of for the future, he cannot but expect every in-vective, that avarice, malice and difap-pointment are able to fuggeft: among

the

the reft he will, no doubt, be charged
with deficiency in his account of the nature of doing bufinefs (as it is called) in
the funds, without the affiftance of a
broker; this being the moft effectual
method to ftop the fale of a work of this
kind : he therefore thinks it his duty pre-
vioufly to acquaint the public, that if the
old Latin maxim be true, which fays,
experientia docet, he is fufficiently mafter
of his fubject * ; and he defires his performance may meet with no further encouragement than it fhall appear to merit by its utility. As fome of the funds
are conftantly open, except on Holidays,
and J———'s almoft always, it will be
very eafy for the purchafers of this little
work, to put it to the proof; and to render it more ufeful, it is printed of fuch a
fize, as to be convenient for the pocket;

---

* The author has loft a genteel fortune, by being
the innocent dupe of the gentlemen of 'Change-
Alley.

for

for if it fhould be found to anfwer the
end propofed, it will become as neceffary
to every merchant, or gentleman, who
has concerns in the funds, as the Tables
of Intereft, or any other calculations
whatever, and will be a ferviceable companion to his pocket-book, the contents
of which, it will preferve from the at-
tacks of Jews and Gentiles.

Among all the various productions of
the prefs, it is amazing that this important
fubject has never been touched, except in
a few fatirical pieces on the fatal year
1720 ; which, though they feverely lafh
the diabolical iniquity of that period, yet
have left no folid inftructions to the public, how to avoid being the dupes of fuch
fort of fchemes, which though carried on
in a lefs confpicuous manner, are yet in
practice to this day. The legiflature indeed, fince that time, have taken every
prudent meafure to put a ftop to the in-

A 4   famous

famous practice of Stock-Jobbing *; but notwithſtanding all the wiſe precautions hitherto taken, only the moſt palpable and glaring frauds have been entirely ſuppreſſed. The Bubbles are indeed burſt, and the Race Horſes of Exchange-Alley long ſince dead, but Bulls, and Bears, ſtill ſubſiſt in their original vigour, and full ſtrength. A gentleman, well known in the city for his long and faithful ſervices in parliament, did, indeed make an attempt ſometime ſince, to cruſh theſe monſters and their keepers; but his ſcheme was rejected, on account of its laying a clog and reſtraint on the buying and ſelling of ſtock: I have therefore great reaſon to hope mine will ſucceed, as it propoſes to leave the method of transferring the funds in the ſame ſituation as at preſent; and only means to make the doing of buſi-neſs at the books change hands, and to

---

* Vid an act of parliament, intitled, An Act for the better preventing the infamous practice of Stock-Jobbing, made in the year 1734.

render

render thofe who have a property in the
funds, the managers of the bufinefs of
buying and felling; which muft be greatly advantageous to the public, and will
at once overturn all Stock-jobbing; for
the extirpation of which (though much
wifhed for) our laws have hitherto proved
ineffectual. The example of a great number of perfons, who from attending the
Bank, the South-Sea, and the India-houfe,
on their own private affairs, have afterwards found it advantageous to commence Brokers and Jobbers, fufficiently
proves the practicability of my defign;
for every one of thefe muft have begun
at firft, with buying and felling Stock for
himfelf, inftead of paying a Broker to do
it; and from thence, finding the expence
of Brokerage faved, has been induced at
length to turn Jobber, from obferving
the vaft crowd of people, who almoft
every transfer-day are to be found, one
day felling, another day buying, and
continually changing the fituation of

A 5   their

their money ; regulating their purfes by
Gazettes, and private letters, as fome do
their diet, and drefs, by barometers.

The art of Stock-Jobbing is not however my principal fubject ; though, for
the fatisfaction of the curious, I fhall give
them a diftinct and clear account of it ;
and therefore, notwithftanding the learn-
ing the method of transferring at the
Books is the high road to Stock-Jobbing,
yet I hope the fenfible reader, who may
only want to lay out his own money, or
his friend's, in the funds, or to fell out
of them, as his various occafions may require, will be content with faving the
brokerage, and will go no further ; for
though he will find every requifite inftruction here for walking the Alley, yet,
as there are every day fome new fcenes
of iniquity contriving behind the curtain,
it is impoffible for me to infure fuccefs ;
which is fcarce ever certain, till thofe
troublefome companions, that generally
attend

attend the innocent, *viz.* Honor, Honefty, and a good Confcience, are intirely
difcarded.

The original defign of employing brokers muft certainly have been for the conveniency of the ladies, for whofe fervice
thefe gentlemen are always ready; (it were
indeed to be wifhed that they had in
general more favourable afpects, and a
genteeler addrefs; for really many an
innocent young lady, who has but juft
heard of 'Change Alley, may reafonably
imagine thefe are the identical Bulls and
Bears fhe has been told of) now the ufe
of thefe gentlemen may eafily be fupplied,
even to the ladies, as I cannot imagine
any lady fo deftitute of relations and
friends, as not to be able to find one
gentleman, who would be fo obliging as
to tranfact her bufinefs for her in the funds,
efpecially when it fhall appear, that it is
the moft fimple and eafy affair in the
whole circle of bufinefs, and attended with
very

very little lofs of time. Nothing is fo
common at prefent, as for executors of
wills (when they are men of underftanding) to transfer a legacy out of the name
of the Teftator into that of the Legatee,
without calling for the affiftance of a
Broker; and why fhould not every gentleman, in the fame manner, affift his
fifter, his coufin, or any other female relation, or friend, when fhe wants to lay out
a fum of money in the funds, or to fell a
fum out of them ? I am certain, that when
I have fully demonftrated not only the
practicability, but likewife the facility,
of rendering this fervice to the ladies,
no gentleman will refufe to devote half
an hour occafionally, to the agreeable
employment of delivering the fair fex
from all connections with this medley of
Barbers, Bakers, Butchers, Shoe-makers,
Plaifterers, and Taylors, whom the mam-
mon of unrighteoufnefs has transformed
into Stock-Brokers. If, in confequence of
a compliance with my plan, thefe gentlemen

men fhould lofe the fair fex, their greateft fupport falls to the ground, fince one
of their principal emoluments arifes from
the management of the fortunes of women.

This branch of their utility once re-
moved, their number will confiderably
diminifh, and their influence on the
public funds be greatly leffened ; and
that this is a thing ardently to be wifhed
for, I believe no man will doubt, when he
is informed, that the gentlemen Stock-
Brokers at this very period of time,
when the author is publifhing this little
treatife, have taken it in their heads
that fome of their fraternity are not fo
good as themfelves ; (which means no
more, than that they are neither fo opu-
lent, nor fo crafty, as the reft) and have
entered into an affociation to exclude
them from J-—'s Coffee-houfe, and for
the future to admit none to the privilege of
facrificing to Plutus, in this his metropo-
litan

litan temple, but by election ; and to fupport themfelves in this famous affociation,
no lefs than one hundred and fifty gentlemen Stock-Brokers have agreed to pay
to the mafter of J——'s the fum of
eight pounds fterling *per annum* each,
amounting in the whole to one thoufand
two hundred pounds, for the privilege
of excluding their poor brethren, and of
affembling about three hours every day
to tranfact only one part of their bufinefs ; the principal part being done at the
public offices, *viz.* the Bank, the South-
Sea-houfe, and the India-Houfe.

Tremble, O ye Gallic hofts ! and thou
Monarch falfely ftyled, *le bein amée*, nor
ever entertain the idle hope of prevail-
ing againft this my native land, for learn
to your aftonifhment, and utter confu-
fion, that her paper credit is arrived to
fuch a height, that her *gentlemen brokers*
alone, (men who live partly on the circulation, but more on the abufe of paper
money

money) can afford to pay twenty-eight
thoufand eight hundred livres of your
money *per annum*, barely for the ufe of
a room; and two or three valets to receive letters and meffages from their
clients, or more properly (in the language
of Drury-lane, which is fynonymous to
that of 'Change-Alley) from their culls.
Think not, O Rome! that with all thy artful fophiftry thou canft invent a more ab-
furd propofition than this, that fome *Devils*
are blacker than others; a propofition,
however, which thefe *gentlemen brokers*
have openly maintained, by their fepara-
tion from their poor brethren.

To return from this neceffary digreffion,
I hope to make it appear, that it is almoft impoffible for a broker, to give any
gentleman, candid and difinterefted advice, when to buy into, or fell out of the
funds; and if I demonftrate this to the
fatisfaction of the public, it will then follow, that after having learned the method
of

of tranfacting bufinefs, and being difpofed to affift the fair fex,the gentleman,and
merchant will have no occafion for a
Stock-Broker; and the public will not
be under a kind of neceffity, of having
every fubfcription towards raifing the annual fupplies, pafs thro' the hands of
thefe legerdemains ; and thus the author's end will be fully anfwered, who
aims at inftructing individuals, for their
profit, and entertaing fociety in general,
by initiating them into the fecrets of
'Change-Alley.

For the benefit of thofe who may ufe
this treatife as a companion to the public
offices, I have inferted a table of the tranf-
fer-days, together with the amount of the
national debt ; and feveral other ufeful
things, which are already publifhed by
themfelves, but without which, this little
book could not properly be completed.

I have only to add, that the diftinguifhed approbation the three former editions

tions of the following sheets have met
with, has induced me to throw aside the
mask; and to venture to mark the title-
page with my real name, disclaiming
henceforth all alliance with the Jewish
race*; and trusting to the candor of the
humane, dispassionate, and benevolent,
for an indulgent reception of the account
I am now to give of myself.

Though the strongest proof of the
truth of what I have advanced on the subject of Stock-jobbing, and of the ex-
actness of the rules I have laid down for
transacting the business of the public
funds, has been given, by the tacit ac-
knowledgement of the gentlemen of the
alley, who have not published the least

---

* In the two first editions a fabulous account of
the author's origin was inserted, which was designed
to divert the gentlemen of the alley, from prema-
turely attributing this piece to any particular pen;
and at the same time to give the public some account
of the birth and progress of modern Stock jobbing.

objection

objection to them, during the fale of three
large impreffions, yet it will no doubt be
a further fatisfaction to the public, to
know that I once frequented Jonathan's ;
and through a fatal error in judgment,
unhappily paid dearly for the experience,
I now offer to the public.

A concern of a public nature in one
branch of the funds firft drew me into
the alley ; and I entered Jonathan's in
the year 1756, folely to fave the expence-
of frequent commiffions, which I found
in a fhort time had amounted to a confiderable fum ; but from a too frequent
attendance, I unhappily fwallowed the
baits that the zealous TUTORS* artfully
laid for my ruin—fuch as frequent in-
finuations, how eafy a thing it was to
grow fuddenly rich, enforced by the
examples of certain Jews, who had formerly been turned adrift in the alley as

* Vide Chap. II.

foon

foon as of age, with the fmall fums of
40 s. five Guineas, or by chance of 50
pounds, from which pitiful beginnings
they had foon acquired fufficient to make
their names fingularly famous, and to
enable them to purchafe every advantage
of Dignity, Eafe, and Elegance.

In the warmth of youth, led on by its
conftant companion, vanity and felf-
conceit, I own that I afpired ; and even
thought that I fhould fpeedily gain—the
riches—the credit—the importance, nay,
even the name of a fecond * * * *. Nor
did I at this period in the leaft conjecture,
that uncommon fubtilty, and a total dif-
regard for the real welfare of my country,
were the foundations on which my fuccefs
in the Alley muft be built.

Examining then, only the flattering
profpect of making a fortune, I tried
every method that the Alley afforded, to
attain this end.—One of which was, fubfcribing much larger fums than I was
                                        able

able to pay in upon, being told, and indeed every year's experience affording inftances, that this is a common practice, the depofit being but fmall, and the gain fometimes very confiderable.—In this attempt, however, I proved extremely unfortunate, having embarked in the public fubfcriptions, at a period of time when, inftead of bearing a premium, they fell below par.

A repetition of annual loffes firft opened my eyes, and engaged me to make a fecret, but exact enquiry into the caufes of the continual fluctuations in the prices of the funds, and I foon found that it did not arife from any critical fituation of public affairs, but from the artful combinations of a fet of men, whofe livelyhood depends on their continual variations; and to whom, it would be death itfelf, if the funds were to remain for any length of time at a fixed price.

This

This truth once difcovered, foon led me on to the knowledge of thofe fcenes of iniquity, that I have now made pub-lic; and in doing which, I declare in the moft folemn manner—*I have nothing extenuated—nor fet down aught in malice.* —So far from it, that I have con-cealed feveral melancholy truths, only from a fear of rendering the very name of 'Change-Alley accurfed to lateft po-fterity.

I have been frequently frightened out of my property in the Alley, and at the Coffee houfes near the Exchange, by men who feemed to me at that time, to be giving me the moft candid advice, dic-tated by the voice of prudence, and con-firmed by the experience of age; yet I have afterwards found, that all this pre-tended friendfhip centered in felf-intereft, and that under the cloak of advifing un-experienced youth, was concealed, the bafe defign of bringing my little ftock to market, to contribute towards a fall, that

that was at that time to take place ; and
to give the fage advifer, an opportunity-
of buying in to advantage.

A feries of misfortunes have fince be-
fallen me, which it would be impertinent
to trouble the public with, but which
were all the confequences of having ven-
tured into the Alley alone—*Meglio è con-
tentarfi che lamentarfi*, is a good leffon, but
very hard to practife, efpecially in a nation, where the knowledge of unmerited
diftrefs, feldom fails of procuring gene-
rous pity, and often diftinguifhed relief.

It has been remarked in print, that the
afperity of a difappointed man has guided
my pen ; had it been known at that time
who was the author, and what caufe I have
had to be fevere, the remark might have
been fpared ; for I have not only loft my
all, but being reduced to the neceffity of
remaining involved in debt to a few individuals, the envenomed tongue of flan-
der has fwelled the fum from hundreds, to
                                    thoufands

thoufands—and this calumny has fprung
from the very fpot, and the very men,
whofe artifices and vile intrigues reduced
me to that neceffity.

The fmall injury done to thefe individuals may be one day repaired ; it is
done in part already—in the mean time,
bleffed with confcious innocence, and re-
gardlefs of the cenfure of diftempered
brains, and malevolent hearts—I fhall
ever reflect with a fecret pleafure, on the
acknowledged good I have done my
country by laying open the iniquity of
ftock-jobbing ; and pointing out a method of tranfacting the bufinefs of the
funds, which if adhered to with becom-
ing refolution and vigor, may fave the
public half a million *per annum*—and
efface the remembrance of my having
failed in a particular branch of bufinefs
connected with the Alley; I know the
world in general are of the late cardinal
de Richelieu's opinion, that, *Malheureux*

et imprudent font deux mots qui fignifient la meme chofe ; but the judicious few, whofe approbation I fhall always endeavour to merit, will judge with more candour and benevolence.

In a word, no particular animofity to any of the gentlemen of the Alley engaged me in this undertaking ; but a firm perfuafion, that the dealing in the funds for time is prejudicial to the public ; and opens a fcene of gaming that annually ruins many families ; and that it is high time to put a ftop to the fatal cataftrophes that are brought upon the ftage of life, by the infernal politics of 'Change-Alley ;—and fo far am I from being enraged at my change of fortune, that I can truly fay with Zeno, *Gratias tibi ago, fortuna, quæ me cogis philofophari*—if therefore I have rendered a few characters at J——'s juftly ridiculous, let it rather be afcribed to a vein for honeft fatire, than to any morofenefs of difpofition occafioned by a reverfe of fortune.

C O N-

CONTENTS.

CHAP. I.

CHAP. II.

CHAP. III.

B   meaning

C H A P. IV.

Giving an account of the method of raifing the annual Supplies granted by Parliament, for defraying the public expences of the State.— Of the manner of fubfcribing, and of buying

and

CHAP. V.

APPENDIX.

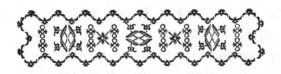

EVERY MAN

HIS OWN

BROKER.

CHAP. I.

Explanation of the Nature of the PUBLIC FUNDS, commonly called the STOCKS.

A T a period of time when the credit of Great Britain is at the higheſt degree of reputation, and her ſecurities for the loan of money are eſteemed the beſt in Europe, not only by her own ſubjects, but likewiſe by

all

all unprejudiced foreigners; a full explanation of the nature of thefe fecurities
merits the attention of all ftrangers, as
well as of the natives of England, on
whom Providence has beftowed any portion of wealth, that is not employed in
commerce, or laid out in landed eftates;
for where will they find fo fafe a repo-
fitory for their money, and on fuch advantageous terms as the public funds of
England afford? Higher intereft may indeed be obtained, but then the fecurity
is not quite fo good.

A company or fociety of merchants
trading to any part of the world, may
fuffer loffes of various kinds, fo as to
leffen the value of the principal fum advanced them, and to oblige them to lower
their dividends; while, on the other
hand, private fecurities are ftill more
hazardous: fo that it neceffarily follows, that the government fecurities
being the fafeft, are the moft advantageous

tageous to lay out money in. But for want of rightly underftanding thefe fecurities, great numbers of perfons, efpecially in the remote parts of the kingdom, lofe the opportunities of engaging in them, and often lend their money, to their great lofs and difappointment, on private fecurities.

Befides the utility of being converfant in the nature of the funds, it will afford a fecret fatisfaction to the public in general, to fee by what eafy methods a free government raifes the large (but neceffary) annual fupplies, for carrying on a heavy and extenfive war, in comparifon of thofe grievous and oppreffive meafures taken in defpotic governments, on the fame emergencies.

Surely the breaft of every Englifhman muft glow with rapture and admiration, when he confiders, that while the unhappy fubjects of the other powers engaged in the prefent war are quite ex-

haufted,

haufted, and thoufands of them totally
ruined, by the demands made on them by
their arbitrary monarchs, he is volun-
tarily contributing towards defraying the
public expences of his country, in a manner that is fo far from being a burden to
him, that, on the contrary, he is ferving
himfelf at the fame time, by lending his
money on parliamentary fecurity; and on
conditions, that though they are not quite
fo profitable as fome others, are yet infured by the credit of the nation, which
exceeds all other fecurity whatever.

The prefent GOVERNMENT FUNDS are,
Three per Cent. Bank reduced Annuities.
Three per Cent. confolidated ditto.
Three per Cent. ditto, 1726.
———————————— ditto, 1751.
Three ½ per Cent. ditto, 1756.
Three ¼ per Cent. ditto, 1758.
Four per Cent. ditto, 1760.
Three per Cent. Subfcription, 1761.
Long Annuities, ——————— ditto.
Lottery Tickets.

Thefe

Thefe are what bufinefs is daily tranfacting in, and are extracted from one of
the printed lifts publifhed by a broker,
which printed lifts are to be had daily,
(about one o'clock in the afternoon) at
any of the brokers offices near the Exchange; and at fome of them may be
feen ftuck up at the windows. I chufe
to diftinguifh the above, from all the
other funds that are inferted in thefe lifts,
or printed in the public news-papers,
under the general name of ftocks, that
the public may be acquainted with the
difference betwixt the funds of particular
focieties, and thofe of the government.

The word STOCK, in its proper figni-
fication, means, that capital in merchan-
dife, or money, which a certain number
of proprietors have agreed to make the
foundation for carrying on an united
commerce, to the equal intereft and advantage of each party concerned, in
B 5 propor

proportion to the fum or fhare contributed by each.

A number of merchants uniting, and applying to the government for an exclufive charter, to prevent others from engaging in the fame commerce, and for a power to raife money by an open fubfcription, in order to form their STOCK, or CAPITAL, are generally denominated COMPANIES.

A conjunction of three or four perfons, who jointly contribute different or equal fums, towards forming a general STOCK to trade with, is called a COPARTNERSHIP ; but the fum of money, or the value of the merchandifes they begin trade with, is ftill properly called their STOCK ; and fo is the CAPITAL with which any fingle man carries on his particular bufinefs.

From this definition of the word it follows, that the application of it to the

lift

lift of government fecurities, here inferted, is highly improper, as they are
abfolutely public D E B T S, and not
STOCKS, for they are all aids granted by
parliament to the government, to enable
it to defray the public expences at fundry
times, and on fundry occafions; and
have been borrowed of the public on the
different conditions contained in the feveral acts of parliament by which they
were raifed; one of which conditions is,
that they fhall be redeemable by parliament, or, in other words, that the parliament referve a power of paying off
thefe fums borrowed of the public.
However, in all this there is not the
leaft fhadow of STOCK or CAPITAL ; but
what amply fupplies the place of it is,
NATIONAL CREDIT, on the ftrength
of which the NATIONAL DEBT has been
contracted; and fo long as the government can keep this CREDIT in reputation,
which it will always be able to do, while
it can find ways and means of paying
the

the annual intereſt of this debt, in the ſame punctual manner that it is paid at preſent, ſo long will NATIONAL CREDIT ſupply the place of STOCK to the government ; and will be a better ſecurity for money than a ſhare in the STOCK of any company whatever, for reaſons which I ſhall give in their proper place : but whether this NATIONAL CREDIT, which is able to engender ſuch large NATIONAL DEBTS, is advantageous or not, to England in general, is a queſtion in politics too nice for us to decide, and foreign to our ſubject.

The STOCK or CAPITAL of our public companies, has been raiſed by authority of parliament ; and by the ſame authority has been confined to a certain ſum ; ſo that as ſoon as the ſum allowed to be raiſed was completed, the number of proprietors was aſcertained and completed alſo, and no perſon whatever could afterwards be admitted on the ſame footing ;

but

but as every proprietor had a power referved to him, his heirs and executors, of
transferring or affigning over his right in
the faid STOCK, to whom he thought proper—this laid the foundation of opening
transfer-books ; and of appointing particular days and hours, for transferring,
affigning over, and accepting ; or, in
other words, for felling and buying of
STOCK.

Every original fhare of a trading company's STOCK muft greatly increafe in
value, in proportion to the advantages
arifing from the commerce they are engaged in ; and fuch is the nature of trade
in general, that it either confiderably increafes, or falls into decline ; and nothing
can be a greater proof of a company's
trade being in a flourifhing condition,
than when their credit is remarkably
good, and the original fhares in their
STOCK will fell at a confiderable premium.

This

This, for inftance, has always been and ftill is, the cafe of EAST INDIA STOCK in particular, not to inftance any other. The prefent price of a fhare of 100*l*. in the company's ftock is 134*l*. The reafon of this advance on what coft the original proprietor only 100*l*. is, that the company, by the profits they have made in trade, are enabled to pay 6*l*. *per annum* intereft or dividend for each 100*l*. fhare.

But then it is uncertain how long they may continue to make fo large an annual dividend, efpecially in time of war ; for feveral circumftances may occur (though it is not likely they fhould) that may moleft their trade in their fettlements, and diminifh their profits ; while, however, there is even a poffibility of this, the premium muft be precarious ; and though it is a great advance on the price given by the original proprietor, yet for a perfon who has money to lay out at prefent, it

is

is not fo advantageous as any of the government annuities ; and for this reafon,
becaufe the company's fhare is intrinfical-
ly worth no more than 100*l.* nor are
they refponfible for any more, confequently the premium has an equal chance
either to rife higher, or totally to fubfide ; and this is the cafe with all fhares
in STOCKS that bear a premium : for
the like imaginary or real advantages,
arifing to any trading company, which
firft advanced the price of the fhares,
may again occur, and contribute to the
raifing them ftill higher ; and the like
real or imaginary loffes, that have happened, and have occafioned the falling
of the price, may again happen, and
produce the fame effect.

Now, the government annuities, and
other fecurities for money, ftand nearly
in the fame light, with refpect to the firft
raifing of the fum granted, as the STOCKS
of companies—that is to fay, the money

is

is raifed by authority of parliament, the
fum is limited; and after the fubfcription
is full, no more contributors can be admitted. In order therefore to remove
the inconveniencies that might arife to
contributors, from being obliged to keep
their money conftantly in the hands of
the government, and that thofe who
have money to lay out, and had not an
opportunity of fubfcribing, may be enabled to purchafe of the fubfcribers; the
fame method has been taken of opening
transfer-books, and of appointing certain days ana hours for transferring and
accepting, or for buying and felling of
the annuities : fo far the government fecurities, and the STOCKS of companies
agree; we fhall now fee wherein they
differ.

As the government are engaged in no
trade, a fhare in their annuities cannot
bear any premium, but what will arife
from the real value of fuch fhare at the

time

time it bears a premium. To illuftrate
this, let us fuppofe that I buy at prefent
100*l.* fhare of 3 *per Cent. Annuities* for
74*l.* the current price, the reafon I buy
it fo low is, that money is worth at
prefent 4½ *per cent. per annum*, and I
am to receive only 3 *per cent.* therefore I give a principal fum in proportion only to the intereft I am to receive.
In a courfe of time the nation enjoys
profound tranquillity, by a lafting and
honourable peace ; and my 100*l.* fhare in
the 3 *per cent. Annuities*, which I bought
for 74*l.* becomes worth 104*l.* or more ;
from whence does this great profit arife ?
not from the uncertain advantages of
trade, but from a natural and probable
event, a public peace, which has
lowered the value of money (the government not being in want of extraordinary fupplies) to fuch a degree, that
more than 3 *per cent.* is not to be obtained
any where, nor even that, on fuch good
fecurity as my fhare in the 3 *per cent.*
Annuities ;

Annuities; therefore I am offered a premium for it, on account of its intrinsic value ; and that the cafe here fuppofed is founded on a precedent, may be proved by referring back to the prices of 3 *per cent. Annuities* in the time of the rebellion*; and comparing them with the price of the fame annuities, before the breaking out of the prefent war.

A time of peace is no fecurity for the premium given on the STOCK of any trading company, becaufe many events may happen as eafy to conjecture as to mention, by which they may fuftain great loffes, and which may occafion the premiums on fhares totally to fubfide. Again, the tranfactions of no fociety whatever are fo open, nor fo foon known, when they concern the public, as the tranfactions of the Britifh government. A number of fatal accidents may be con-

---

* Vid. the Gentleman's Magazine for Nov. 1745.

cealed

cealed for a long time in private focieties ;
but a rupture with a foreign power,
which is almoft the only thing in time of
peace, that ought to affect the price of
the government fecurities, is prefently
known; and confequently, as foon as
the rumor of a war is fpread, the perfon
who has given a premium on annuities,
has an opportunity of felling at a fmall
lofs, 4 or 5 *per cent.* but whenever a long
concealed misfortune that has happened
to any trading fociety, comes to be di-
vulged, or that the fociety takes any un-
expected meafures, the fall on the fhares
in the STOCK of fuch a fociety, may be
20 or 30 *per cent.* in one day*.

Again, the difference between the go
vernment annuities and the STOCKS of
trading companies, when bought at a
difcount, (or under par) is very great;

---

* Witnefs the fall on India Stock, owing to the
fudden reduction of intereft from 8 to 6 *per cent.*
about the year 1755.

for

for fhould it ever happen, that the fhares
in the CAPITAL or STOCK of any fociety, fell confiderably under par, it may
reafonably be concluded, that the finances
of the fociety are in a bad condition, and
their trade on the decline ; but the government annuities felling at a great difcount is only a proof of the increafe of
the value of money, which will always
be in proportion to the demands of the
ftate for it.

Thus he who, at the beginning of the
war would willingly have lent the government his money at $3\frac{1}{2}$ *per cent.* will
not now part with it under $4\frac{1}{2}$, becaufe
the wants of the ftate continuing, have
raifed the value of money ; but this is
no argument, either that the finances of
the ftate are in a bad condition, or that
its credit is on the decline.   On the contrary, I do not know of any public event
(the rebellion excepted) which has in
                                    the

the leaft weakened public credit, nor
which ought to have caufed any great
variation in the prices of the government
fecurities; and here I muft add a few
words, which I am certain will greatly
offend the *moneyed men*, but may not be
difagreeable to the public.

I am humbly of opinion then, that a
method might be found out, of keeping
the funds from thefe perpetual variations,
(except in cafe of an actual formidable
invafion, the total deftruction of our
maritime force, or any other more re-
markable cataftrophe than any that has
happened this war) and of fupplying
the government with what money they
want, on the fame terms at the latter
end of a war, as at the beginning, provided the war does not laft fo long as to
make a real fcarcity of money; which,
I think, has not been the cafe in the prefent war, as appears by the immediate
filling

filling of every subscription for raising the annual supplies.*

I confess it to be a Herculean labour, but yet it is to be accomplished,—if the influence the brokers have over the *moneyed men*, is once destroyed, which it is hoped this little piece will in part, if not totally effect.

The BANK ANNUITIES, and other government securities, inserted at the beginning of this chapter, together with the following CAPITALS or STOCKS of companies, and their Annuities and Bonds, make up the list that is commonly inserted, with their several prices, in the public news-papers, under the general title of STOCKS.

---

* The subscription towards raising the supplies granted by parliament, for the service of the present year, amounting to thirteen millions, it is said, was filled by ten gentlemen, merchants of London.

Bank

Bank Stock 4 ½ per Cent.
South Sea Stock 3 ½ per Cent.
India Stock 6 per Cent.
South Sea Annuities 3 per Cent.
India Annuities 3 per Cent.
India Bonds 5 per Cent.

These are securities nearly equal to the government annuities, and far preferable to the securities of any private societies whatever. They are all transferrable, or saleable, without any restraint or difficulty, as will appear in Chap. 3. wherein the method of doing it is fully explained.

Having thus given a succinct account of the public funds, in a style which I hope will be intelligible to the meanest capacity; I have only to add a few remarks that naturally arise out of the explanation I have given of them, and which I hope will not be entirely useless to the public.

It

It appears then, that the government
fecurities of England are abfolutely preferable to all others whatever.

That fnares in the Stokcs of the public companies of England are nearly
equal to the government fecurities, and
far preferable to the fecurities given
by private focieties, or particular perfons.

That fhares in annuities bought at a
great difcount, that is to fay, greatly
under par, are the cheapeft and moft advantageous to the purchafer; and confiderably more profitable than than any
Stocks bought at a high premium.
Becaufe the probability of the premium
(given on any Stock) totally fubfiding,
is infinitely greater, than that the low
price at prefent given for 3 *per Cent. Annuities*, fhould fall much lower; and
there is a greater probability of their
rifing, and a greater likelihood of its
continuance, than there is, that the premium now given on any Stock fhould
rife

rife much higher, or continue fo high as
it is, for any number of years : therefore
fhares in Stocks that bear a premium,
are the deareft ; and fhares in funds or
annuities under par, the cheapeft to purchafe.

That perfons who have fubfcribed; or
bought into, the 3 *per cent.* or other government annuities fome years ago, at a
much higher price than the prefent, ought
not to fell out, unlefs on an unavoidable
emergency ; let what will be the tempta-
tions offered by brokers to engage them
to do it ; fince, in their cafe, they will
fcarce better themfelves by any new fubfcription ; and fince, if they were to offer
to fell, they would always find buyers,
whofe defire of buying what they want
to part with, plainly makes a doubt of
the matter ; for it fhews that the purchafers (or their brokers for them) have as
good an opinion of the annuities the fellers are going to part with at a great lofs,

as

as they have of any new fubfcription*:
therefore, unlefs in a cafe of neceffity, never remove your money at a lofs ; but
wait patiently till the fituation of public
affairs has brought it back to the price
you gave, or a much higher ; and never
believe any idle rumors of bad news, fo
far as to let them frighten you out of
your intereft in the government fecurities ; for thofe fecurities have not for
many years, nor are likely again, to be
in any real danger.

Finally, That the man who wants to
engage you to be continually changing
the fituation of your money, is influenced
by fome private motive : for which reafon, never follow his advice, unlefs you
are a JOBBER yourfelf.

---

* It is the Broker's bufinefs to throw out all poffible baits to engage people to be continually changing from one fund to another, for this brings grifts
to his mill : every movement of this kind, producing frefh commiffion money.

C H A P.

CHAP. II.

Of the Myftery and Iniquity of STOCK-JOBBING
in all its various branches.

✤✤✤✤✤ GIVE this account of STOCK-
✤ I ✤ JOBBING the fecond place in
✤ ✤ this little piece, becaufe it may
✤✤✤✤✤ prove an agreeable relaxation
to the mind after fo dry a fubject as that
of the STOCKS ; and likewife becaufe it is
neceffary to give an account of the various branches of STOCK JOBBING before I
infert my general inftructions for tranfacting the feveral parts of the bufinefs of
the public funds.

It will be neceffary to premife, that the
iniquitous art of STOCK-JOBBING has
fprung, like a great many other abufes,
out of the beft of bleffings, LIBERTY,
which the Englifh nation, to its immortal
honour be it recorded, is ever ftudious to

C 2   extend

extend the benign influence of, to foreigners, as well as its own natives.

It will be allowed, there is no good thing on earth that may not be abufed; but this is no argument that the good, out of which evil is produced, is the lefs valuable : On the contrary, it only aggra vates the guilt of thofe who are fo corrupt as to make even virtue itfelf, ferve the caufe of vice.

What judgment muft pofterity form of the prefent age, when they read, that in almoft every inftance we turned liberty into licentioufnefs; that, from that invaluable branch of it, the liberty of the prefs, arofe the moft licentious abufes of it,—an inundation of fcurrility,—obfcenity,—and low humour,—corrupting the morals of beardlefs youth and hoary age, and with the affiftance of artful colourings, and the fanction of the facred robe*, viti-

* Vid. T——m S——y, in 4 vols. faid to be wrote by a celebrated clergyman.

ating

ating the tafte of Britons to fuch a degree,
that thefe productions were made the tefts
of mens knowledge in the Belle-Lettres,
and the ftandards of all polite converfation ?

In fhort, that at the fame period of
time, from the free liberty granted to all
foreigners to buy into, and fell out of,
our public funds, the diabolical art of
STOCK-JOBBING arrived at its meridian
of iniquity, which brings me back to my
fubject, from which I find I have wan-
dered not a little ; and happy it is for my
readers, that I have neither met with a
Hot chefnut, or Slawkenberg's Story of
Long Nofes, for if I had, heaven knows
when their curiofity would have been fatisfied as to STOCK-JOBBING, which muft
have given place to the reigning Shandean
tafte.

The great concerns which foreigners,
and efpecially the Dutch, have had in our
funds for more than half a century paft,

C 3   demon-

demonſtrate the goodneſs of the Engliſh
fecurities in preference to all others ; and
that the manner in which the buſineſs of
them is tranſacted, is the plaineſt and moſt
free from all difficulties and embarraſſ-
ments ; and likewiſe that the punctual
payment of fmall intereſt is, by all prudent people, more to be prized, than the
vain promiſes of much larger intereſt,
where there is not a probability of its being punctually paid, if it is ever paid at
all *

Now, the Dutch and other foreigners
having ſo large an intereſt in our public
funds, has given riſe to the buying and
felling of them for time, by which is to
be underſtood, the making of contracts
for buying and felling againſt any certain
period of time ; ſo that the transfer at the
public offices is not made at the time of

---

* The payment of the intereſt of many of the
French loans is at preſent either poſtponed, or totally
ſtopt.

making

making the contract; but at the time ftipulated in the contract for transferring it; and this has produced modern STOCK-JOBBING, as I fhall prefently have occafion to fhew.

Nothing could be more juft or equitable than the original defign of thefe contracts, nor nothing more infamous than the abufe that has been, and ftill is made of it.

The original defign of thefe contracts, I imagine, was, that a Dutchman, or any other foreigner, having occafion to buy into, or fell out of, our public funds, and being informed by his correfpondent at London, of an advantageous opportunity of doing either, might be enabled to embrace fuch opportunity, by writing to his friend to contract immediately for any quantity of STOCK againft fuch a time, before which time, he might fend his correfpondent a remittance, if it did not fuit him to do it immediately; whereas, if it

C 4   were

not for thefe contracts, the transfer (in the
common courfe of bufinefs) being to be
made, and the money to be paid at the
fame time, if it did not fuit his correfpondent to advance it, nor him to remit it, the
opportunity would be loft; and again, that
his correfpondent might not be prevented
from taking advantage of a favorable
opportunity either of buying or felling
for him, by waiting the arrival of powers
of attorney, or other neceffary inftru-
ments, authorifing him to tranfact the bufinefs at the offices.

This is the fhorteft and moft probable
account I am able to give of the original
intent of contracts for felling Stock for
time—the four principal times, for which
contracts or bargains are made, are February, May, Auguft, and November,
and thefe are called in 'Change Alley, the
Refcounter* fettlings. The correfpon-
dents

* In the former editions of this work, the Author declared himfelf at a lofs for the etymology of
the

dents of such foreigners as are concerned in
our funds being generally merchants; these
having

the word Refcounter, which he is now enabled to
give a full account of, for which the public are indebted to an honourable gentleman residing in
Holland in a public capacity, who has been so
obliging as to write the following letter to the
author.

'SIR,

' I thank you for your book, which has made me
' understand what before I had not the least notion
' of.—In your 30th page, in the note, you say you
' are at a loss for the etymology of Refcounter. I
' shall take the liberty to give you the meaning of
' the said word, as used among Dutch merchants,
' by which you may see how it has been adopted in
' the Alley.—'Tis customary with Dutch merchants
' who have mutual dealings and running accounts,
' and who live in the same town, to give a receipt
' at the bottom of a bill of parcels, or invoice of
' goods sold to each other, in these words, *solvit per*
' *rescontre*, which is understood to mean, that the
' value of such invoice has been adjusted in accounts
' current between them, even small notes of hand,
' or assignations (as the Dutch call them) are thrown
' into these accounts current.—When payments
' are made otherways, they say, *solvit per banco*,

C 5   *solvit*

having no fpare time, have recourfe to Brokers, who make thefe contracts for them ;
and the method is thus : a Broker declares
that he has a commiffion to buy (fuppofe
in the month of March) 1000 *l. 3 per Cent.
Annuities* for the Refcounters in May ;
and it is not long before he finds a brother,
who declares he has a commiffion to fell
1000 *l.* for the fame time ; after agreeing
then on the price, the one marks down
in his book, fold to Zerubabel Ambufh
1000 *l. 3 per Cent. Annuities* for May ; and
the other, bought of Jemmy Sly 1000 *l. 3
per Cent. Annuities* for that time ; and thus
the bargain is finifhed 'till May : but the
principal, or perfon who employed them, is
not declared on either fide ; as it ought to

‘ *folvit per caffa, folvit per wiffel,* &c. this denotes
‘ the different manner in which payments have been
‘ made, and facilitates the tracing of any articles
‘ that may be difputed. I fhall be glad if this throws
‘ any light upon the etymology of the word Ref-
‘ counter, as ufed with you, and am,

‘ Your moft humble Servant, &c.’

be

be ; of which hereafter, when we come to treat of the laws in force refpecting Brokers.

Now, were this proceeding to ftop here, it would only anfwer the original defign, (except in the laft mentioned particular) and would be fo far juft and equitable ; but the mifchief of it is, that under this fanction of felling and buying the funds for time for foreigners, Brokers and others buy and fell for themfelves, without having any intereft in the funds they fell, or any cafh to pay for what they buy, nay even without any defign to transfer, or accept, the funds they fell or buy for time.

The bufinefs thus tranfacted, has been declared illegal by feveral acts of parliament, and is the principal branch of STOCK-JOBBING ; and the genuine fource to which we are indebted for that variety of Private Letters from Holland—Secret Intelligences, — Important

Events,

Events, — Bloody Engagements, — Flat-
bottomed Boats, — Spanish Fleets, joining with French, — Difference with foreign
Powers, — Death of a certain great Per-
sonage, a Principal in the present War —
Breaking out of the Plague — Alterations
in the Ministry — and that infinity of *et
ceteras*, of the same kind, which are to
be found every week inserted in some of
our papers, and contradicted in others ;
but which are all subservient to the great
purpose of promoting the trade of
STOCK-JOBBING.

In order to prove that STOCK-JOB-
BING produces a great variety of articles
in the news-papers, as well as rumours
and reports in coffee-houses, and the
better to explain the whole mystery of
this art, I shall endeavour to give a
clear account of STOCK-JOBBERS ; and
shall distinguish the different sorts of
them ; and convince the public, that it
lies under a great error, when it confines
the

the contemptuous term of STOCK-JOBBERS, wholly to STOCK-BROKERS; an error, however, which of late has univerfally prevailed ; for whenever STOCK-JOBBING has been brought upon the carpet, either in periodical effays, or upon the ftage, the characters are defcribed either as Jewifh or Chriftian Brokers, and thofe of the meaneft and fhabbieft fort, except in a very fenfible little effay in the Imperial Magazine for Auguft 1760, in which the author very juftly introduces fome characters in a higher ftation of life.

STOCK-JOBBERS may be divided into three different forts.

The firft are foreigners, who have property in our funds, with which they are continually JOBBING.

The fecond are our own gentry, merchants, and tradefmen, who likewife have
property

property in the funds, with which they
job, or, in other words, are continually
changing the fituation of their property,
according to the periodical variations of
the funds, as produced by the divers in-
cidents that are fuppofed either to leffen,
or increafe the value of thefe funds, and
occafion fudden rifes or falls of the current price of them.

The third, and by far the greateft
number, are STOCK-BROKERS, with very
little, and often with no property at all
in the funds, who job in them on credit,
and tranfact more bufinefs in the feveral
government fecurities in one hour, without having a fhilling of property in any
one of them, than the real proprietors of
thoufands tranfact in feveral years.*

Foreigners,

---

* A few years fince a STOCK-BROKER wanted
to prove a debt of 100 *l.* under a commiffion of
bankruptcy; the reft of the creditors objected to
it; and he was afked, how his debt arofe? he re-
plied,

Foreigners, who have property in our
funds, and are JOBBERS, are the moſt

---

plied, it was for brokerage, for buying and ſelling
STOCKS for the bankrupt. This was thought very
extraordinary, as the time of tranſacting this
buſineſs for him, was the very time when he was
greatly indebted to his ſeveral creditors ; and con-
ſequently it was ſuppoſed, that if he had ſuch
a property in the funds as to enable him to owe his
broker 100*l.* merely for commiſſion, which is no
more than 2*s.* 6*d. per Cent.* he had no occaſion to
remain in debt. In ſhort, he was not allowed to
come in as a creditor, upon which he very fooliſhly
commenced a ſuit againſt the parties concerned ;
and was moſt juſtly nonſuited. It appeared upon
the trial, that he had bought and ſold for the bankrupt, of various government ſecurities, about
70,000*l.* in one quarter of a year, that is, from one
reſcounters to another: and that the bankrupt at
this time had not, nor could not be ſuppoſed to
have, 100*l.* property in any one of the funds.
As the whole tranſaction therefore was STOCK-
JOBBING, and expreſsly contrary to act of parliament,
the bringing ſuch a cauſe into a court of judicature
was reckoned a moſt extraordinary piece of aſſu-
rance ; and caſt that odium and contempt on the
gentlemen of 'Change-Alley, who attended in be-
half of their brother, that they juſtly merited.

guilty

guilty of injuftice to the public of any
of the parties concerned in this iniquitous
practice : becaufe they are often men of
credit, and fometimes of authority, in
their own countries, which are perhaps
in alliance with us in time of war, and
therefore whatever falfe news they fend
over, to anfwer their private JOBBING
accounts, is not fo foon fufpected, nor
its falfehood fo eafily detected, as thofe
which are made at home : for inftance,
if a magiftrate of a renowned city, whofe
government is in alliance, or at peace
with us, fends over a letter to his correfpondent at London, in which he affures
him, that on fuch a day, and at fuch a
place, the French gained a confiderable
advantage over the allied army ; and
backs his intelligence with orders to this
correfpondent to fell out 1000, or 2000*l.*
of his property in the funds, becaufe he
thinks this advantage gained by the
French may prove detrimental to the
affairs of England, and endanger or at
leaft

leaft greatly leſſen, the value of our
funds, the public becomes immediately
affected by this letter, at leaft ſuch part
of it as have concerns in the funds; for
it is ſhewn publicly upon 'Change,
and proper care taken to ſpread the
intelligence of his having ordered
STOCK to be ſold out; the gentlemen of
the Alley (who know the meaning of
ſuch letters, ſome of which arrive with
every mail) receive the intelligence dif-
ferently, as it ſuits their different in-
tereſts; thoſe who want the STOCKS to
fall, take the utmoſt pains to propagate
the intelligence; and to enlarge on the
authority, credit, and veracity of the
letter-writer; and to put the finiſhing
ſtroke to this ſcene of STOCK-JOBBING
policy, they immediately ſend a copy of
the letter to the printers of ſome of the
news-papers, and at the ſame time ad-
viſe all their employers to ſell. The
unſuſpecting public, on reading the news,
are eaſily inclined to believe it, becauſe
it

it comes from a friendly quarter. Were it taken from the Bruffels Gazette, it would of courfe be a falfehood ; but as it is a private letter from one of our friends, who, we may fuppofe would fooner give the moft favourable, than the worft account of things, 'tis univerfally credited. " The patriot fighs for his " bleeding countrymen—the malecon- " tent exclaims againft the meafures of " the miniftry, and damns German Prin- " ces, and German Politics." The an- tiquated maiden, who fubfifts on the annual income of her property in the funds, and the mifer, who always hated paper-money, tremble alike for their property, and reafon thus with them- felves. — " STOCKS are fallen on this " news 3 per Cent. perhaps to-morrow " it may be worfe, and the following day " worfe ftill; better fell before all is loft. " Alas ! poor Old England, this na- " tional debt will be thy ruin one day " or other ; well, land cannot run away,
" I'll

" I'll e'en go into the city and fell, be-
" fore it is too late." With the fame
idle fears, hundreds run to the Alley,
and fell on the credit of fuch fort of
letters. The next day, the gentlemen
Brokers of the oppofite party, who
want the STOCKS to rife, take care to
have this intelligence contradicted : then,
thofe who have fold, fee their error,
and want to buy in again, which if
they do, they are obliged to give an
advanced price ; the fhock is over ;
and the funds have recovered their former price ; or perhaps a true piece of
good news, has raifed them much higher
than they were, before our falfe friend's
letter was made public. To complete
this example of the mifchief that
STOCK JOBBING foreigners make, and
which many of my readers will allow
is no exaggeration, there remains only
to inform the public, that this worthy
magiftrate, at the time he fends this
news, and orders a 1000l. to be fold

out

out, fends private orders to his Broker
to buy in 50,000*l*. (when his news has
effected a fall) in order to fettle his
JOBBING account in the Alley; for,
alas, poor man! he had engaged to
deliver 50,000*l*. for May refcounters,
which he had fold on fpeculation at a
low price, without being poffeffed of it;
but it matter'd not, " the French at the
" beginning of the fpring, would fend
" 150,000 men into Germany, the king
" of Pruffia would be crufhed before
" May ;" and the 50,000*l*. confequently
might be bought at a much lower price
than he had fold it at, and the account
be adjufted greatly to his advantage.
Thus embarked, he naturally wifhes deftruction to Old England, which, as a
foreigner, but more efpecially as one of
that nation, whofe God is felf-intereft*,
is

---

* A French Author fays, that in Holland the
Demon of gold, being crowned with tobacco
leaves,

is not fo much to be wondered at;
" but oh! fhame, horrid fhame, to
" Englifhmen, ever to be engaged in
" contracts which muft make them
" wifh misfortunes may befal their
" country." For once, however, the
poor magiftrate finds his error, no mif-
fortune has really happened to England,
or her renowned ally ; and therefore he
is obliged, as we have feen, to forge a
piece of bad news, to lower the Stocks
as much as he can ; but the mifchief
not having happened that he had formed
in his brain, his accompt is obliged to
be finally adjufted greatly to his difadvantage.

---

leaves, and feated on a throne of cheefe, is publicly adored.—I fuppofe he had obferved, that
the Dutch make the *fummum bonum* of this life,
to confift in having plenty of thefe three articles,
gold, tobacco, and cheefe.

Numberlefs

Numberlefs inftances of this fpecies of
STOCK-JOBBING might be given ; but
the author hopes, that this one will fuffice
to give the common reader a diftinct idea
of the nature of it ; and the judicious
will need no key to realize this, or any
other characters he may have occafion to
defcribe.

The fecond clafs of STOCK-JOBBERS,
are our own countrymen, of almoft every
rank and denomination ; and as fome of
very high rank amongft us are extremely
addicted to common gaming, it is no
wonder to find them deeply engaged in
the more refined and artful games of the
Alley. Thefe do more or lefs prejudice
to the public, in proportion to their ftation and influence, and the fums they
for.

Thus, for inftance, one who enjoys
any confiderable poft in the nation, by
which he may be fuppofed to have the
earlieft intelligence of all events that can
tend

tend either o raife, or fall the STOCKS,
and whofe veracity, or rather whofe honor, will not admit the fuppofition
of his propagating a falfehood.—If he
fhould be a JOBBER, and in order to fettle
a great accompt in the Alley to his advantage, fhould for once fwerve from the
truth, and, upon his honor, report a
piece of news to be true, which is not,
will do as much mifchief for a fhort time,
as the foreigner already mentioned. A-
gain, the General of an army, or the Com-
mander in chief of a fleet, who are JOB-
BERS, fhould they have a great deal depending in the Alley, and their account
fhould ftand fo as to require a fall of the
STOCKS,—if they difappoint the fanguine
expectations of the public, and inftead
of gaining or purfuing a victory, only juft
do as much, as will barely fave their lives
at a court-martial, becaufe they will not,
by a complete victory, raife thofe funds
they want to fall—are STOCK-JOBBERS,
who do the public a double prejudice ;

firft,

firft, by not performing their duty in the important fervices they are entrufted with; and, fecondly, by caufing a fall in the funds that may alarm, and frighten many of the adventurers in the funds, and engage them to fell out their property to a difadvantage.

I am fenfible that it will appear an ab-furd fuppofition to imagine, that perfons in fuch high ftations fhould be capable of a neglect of duty on fuch bafe motives: and indeed I will not poffitively affert, that we have ever had an inftance of it: but, at the fame time, give me leave to obferve,—that both ancient and mo-dern hiftory, furnifhes us with many re-markable inftances of the bafeft actions being committed by men of high rank, and the moft exalted ftations in govern-ment, for fmaller pecuniary advantages than thofe which might arife in the cafes here fuppofed,—and that, the gain of twenty or thirty thoufand pounds, may, with the

covetous

covetous, or prodigal, in high life, out-
weigh the lofs of honor, or a difgracing
fentence from a court-martial*.

Let us now proceed to the monied man,
who has no other influence nor authority,
but that, which his cafh gives him ; but
who, with the advantage of having a current capital of ten or twelve thoufand
pounds, becomes a man of great confequence in the Alley, and has no fmall influence on that part of the public, who
have any concern with the funds.

He deals in the Alley with a defign to
double this fum, by a much fpeedier method than by a flavifh, tedious application,
to the fmall profits of merchandifing.

---

* It muft certainly be of great advantage to any
ftate, to examine ftrictly what gaming connections of
any kind the perfon has, who is a candidate for the
higheft pofts in a kingdom ; for who fo likely to take
a bribe, as he who lofes thoufands in an hour, and
pays his debts of honor,—like a man of honor.

D   He

He has experienced the furprifing effects of
STOCK JOBBING already, having increaf-
ed his patrimony, by a diligent attendance
in the Alley, from two, to twelve thoufand
pounds; and is now become an adept in
the art; he has not a friend or acquain-
tance whom he does not attempt to convince of his fuperior judgment in the
funds; and that he has the earlieft and moft
authentic accounts from different parts of
the world (by private letters) of all events
that concern the nation, and can any ways
affect the funds. Sometimes he is well
affured, that we are at the eve of a peace,
and advifes all his friends to buy STOCK.
This of confequence procures a rife, which
was what he wanted, being a * BULL of
twenty thoufand 3 per Cent. Annuities; and
by

---

* A Bull is the name by which the gentlemen of
'Change Alley, chufe to call all perfons, who contract
to buy any quantity of government fecurities, without
an intention or ability to pay for it; and who confequently

by propagating the report of an approaching peace he has engaged so many people
to buy, that he has raised the price, and by
this means has got rid of his twenty thousand at 2 or 3 *per Cent.* profit.

Another time he has just received intelligence that the Spaniards are on the point-
of joining the French, and will immediately assist them with a formidable fleet:
he therefore advises all his friends to sell
out, for STOCKS will fall 10 *per Cent.* and
if they sell out now, they will have a fine

oppor-

---

quently are obliged to sell it again, either at a profit, or
a loss, before the time comes, when they have contracted to take it. Thus a man who in March, buys
in the Alley 40,000*l.* 4 *per Cent. Annuities* 1760, for the
refcounters in May, and at the same time is not worth
10*l.* in the world, or, which is the same thing, has
his money employed in trade, and cannot really take
the *annuities* so contracted for, is a BULL, till such
time as he can discharge himself of his heavy burden
by selling it to another person, and so adjusting the
account ; which, if the whole house be BULLS, he
will

opportunity of buying in again, much lower. To confirm his belief of the intelligence he has received, and to make his practice correspond with his opinion, he really sells out five or six thousand pounds, which he has ready for this occasion in some of the funds; his unsuspecting friends being by this means convinced of

---

will be obliged to do, at a considerable loss ; and in the interim, (while he is betwixt hope and fear, and is watching every opportunity to ease himself of his load on advantageous terms, and when the fatal day is approaching that he must sell, let the price be what it will,) he goes lowering up and down the house, and from office to office ; and if he is asked a civil question, he answers with a surly look and by his dejected gloomy aspect, and morosenels, he not badly represents the animal he is named after.

A BULL is likewise a person who has bought and actually paid for, a large quantity of any new fund, commonly called *Subscription*, while there is no more than one or two payments made on it, but who is unable to pay in the whole of the sum, and consequently is obliged to part with it again, before the next pay day.

the

of the truth of what he has related, follow
his example, and univerfally fpread the
report ; fo that the great numbers of perfons who are induced thereby to fell, and
the coldnefs of thofe who want to buy,
confiderably lowers the price, which is
all the good man aims at, who at this time
is a BEAR * in the Alley of thirty thoufand
pounds

---

* A BEAR, in the language of 'Change-Alley, is
a perfon who has agreed to fell any quantity of the
public funds, more than he is poffeffed of, and often
without being poffeffed of any at all, but which never-
thelefs he is obliged to deliver againft a certain time ;
before this time arrives, he is continually going up
and down feeking whom, or, which is the fame thing,
whofe property he can devour ; you will find him in
a continual hurry ; always with alarm, furprize and
eagernefs painted on his countenance; greedily fwal-
lowing the leaft report of bad news ; rejoicing in mifchief, or any misfortune that may bring about the
wifhed for change of falling the STOCKS, that he may
buy in low, and fo fettle his account to advantage.
He is eafily diftinguifhed from the BULL, who is ful-
ky and heavy, and fits in fome corner in a gloomy
melancholy pofture ; whereas the BEAR, with mea-

D 3   ger,

pounds of fome of the ANNUITIES or
STOCKS which he has now had an opportunity of buying to adjuft his account
with, on much better terms than he
could have bought them, if it had not
been for this news ; and the lofs he has
fuftained on the 5 or 6000*l.* (which he
fold as a blind) is trifling, in comparifon
of the lofs he has prevented, or perhaps

---

ger, haggard looks, and a voracious fiercenefs in his
countenance, is continually on the watch, feizes on all
who enter the Alley, and by his terrific weapons
of groundlefs fears,—and falfe rumours,—frightens
all around him out of that property, he wants to buy :
and is as much a monfter in nature, as his brother
brute in the woods. The author hopes this, and the
foregoing note, will be carefully attended to, as he
fhall often have occafion to mention thefe two brutes in
human form ; and will not give any further defcription of them, imagining this fufficient, not only
for the underftanding this little treatife, but likewife
fully to defcribe them, and the difference between
them, to all tolerable judges of phyfiognomy, who
may hereafter meet with them in their walks through
'Change-Alley.

of

of the profit he has made, on clofing his
STOCK-JOBBING account. To finifh
this character, let me inform the public,
that the letter of intelligence on which
this fcene of action is founded, was made
abroad, by the gentleman's defire, and
according to his own form, to anfwer
this very end. Nay, if that could not be
contrived for want of a correfpondent
abroad, it was very eafy to fupply that
defect, by means of any German, French
or Dutch clerk, in the compting-houfe
at home.

Next to this clafs of Jobbers follows a
whole group of characters, who are tradefmen, and fhopkeepers of various kinds;
and who may reafonably be fuppofed to
have laid out their capitals, in purchafing
the ftocks of their feveral warehoufes and
fhops; and therefore can never have any
great quantity of cafh in the funds. To
fay the truth, the greateft part of them
have not a fhilling of property in any

D 4   one

one of the government fecurities. Thefe
men therefore walk the Alley, on credit
and honor; that is to fay, as they are
known to be fubftantial tradefmen, and
men whofe word (in the city ftile) is as
good as their bond, they have nothing
to do but to give orders to a Broker,
to buy them 50 or 60,000l. of any of the
funds, for any particular time, or to fell
the fame fum. This order is executed
as foon as the tradefman has affured the
Broker, that he will act upon honor, and
pay any lofs that may arife upon clofing
the account.

We will fuppofe for a moment then,
that one of thefe tradefmen is a coffee-
houfe politician; and has lately in his
own imagination found out, that fome
connections the adminiftration are on the
point of entering into abroad, or fome
meafures they are likely to take at home,
will tend to raife the STOCKS confiderably, which now bear a low price. Fired
with

with the idea of greater gain, and much
eafier to be procured, than any he could
hope for, by an attendance on his fhop,
he quits it, and runs to the Alley, where
he gives orders to buy 70,000*l*. *3 per
Cent. Annuities*, for the following refcounters: when this is done, he returns
home fully fatisfied with his fuperior
judgment; and to make his cafe the
better, he once more quits his fhop ear-
lier than ufual in the evening, to entertain
his fellow citizens at fome punch-houfe
or tavern, with an harangue on the great
advantages we are likely to gain over the
enemy in a fhort time ; and affures them,
that now or never is the time, to get
money by buying STOCKS ; and if luckily
there is a town befieged by England or
its allies, he is ready to lay nine to one
all round the room, that it is in our hands
before the 30th of Auguft (the time his
account is to be fettled). This fatal day
however advances, and no fortunate news
arrives.—The good Broker waits on his

D 5   friend

friend to acquaint him that the time is drawing nigh; and defires to know what is to be done with the 70,000*l.* Annuities, which he well knows the tradefman never intends to take. " The young citizen " replies by enquiring, if there is no " news with the laft mail, no rumor of a " peace, nor no advantage gained over " the enemy. To which the feemingly " melancholy Broker anfwers, No, dear " Sir, quite the contrary; there is a re- " port that we have loft a battle; and that " there will foon be a change of the " miniftry. A change of the miniftry ! " heaven forbid ! then we are all ruined. " And do you really believe it, Mr. " Longfhanks ? Yes, Sir, upon my " honor, I am afraid it is too true, for " they are all turned fellers to day, and " 3 *per cent's.* are fallen 4 *per cent.* below " the price you bought at ; and they fay " the houfe are *bulls* for the refcounters. " The devil they are, Sir; why what " would you advife me to do then ? I

fhall

" fhall lofe finely I fuppofe ! Do, Sir,
" why I think,—I think I would ad-
" vife you to fell and clofe the account,
" for I am afraid you will only make
" it worfe by ftaying till the laft day.
" 'Tis a little unlucky to be fure, but
" we fhall recover it again, and more
" to it, next refcounters.   Shall I fell,
" Sir ?—Why yes, the firft lofs is beft,
" and pray let me have the account,
" that I may difcharge it, for I fhall be
" out of town on the fettling day."
In a fhort time Mr. Longfhanks returns;
and thus continues the fcene: " Well,
" Sir, I have done it at laft at $1\frac{1}{8}$, I be-
" lieve the people are mad.—I thought
" I fhould never have got it done ;—they
" are all fellers to a man ;—Well, I muft
" make all the hafte I can to Sir Solo-
" mon Wronghead, for he is a BULL of
" half a million ; and I muft advife him
" to fell before things grow worfe.
" Here, Sir, is your account.

Bought

Mar. 31, 1761.

| Bought for Mr. Deputy Dowlas, 70,000 *l.* 3 *per Cent. Annuities* for the refcounters in May, a 81 ⅛. | Sold for Mr. Deputy Dowlas, 70,000 *l.* 3 *per Cent. Annuities* for May refcounters, a 76 ⅝. |

" The difference, Sir, is 4½ *per Cent.*
" which comes to —— £ 3150 0 0
" and my commiffion for ⎫
" buying and felling at ⅛ ⎬ 87 10 0
" *per Cent.* is — — ⎭

                    £ 3237 10 0

" Well, Sir, you will write a receipt, and
" I will give you a draught on my
" Banker for the money.   Pardon me,
" Sir, you know this whole tranfaction
" is exprefsly againft act of parliament *,
" and therefore we never give recepts,

---

* Vid. an Act 7th Geo. II. intitled, An Act the better to prevent the infamous practice of Stock-Jobbing.

                              " nor

" nor take any ; all is upon honour, Sir,
" which you will know by and by, when
" I have a large balance to pay you.
" Well, Sir, how ſhall I write you in
" the draught ? pray what is your chri-
" ſtian name ? Oh, Sir, you need not be
" particular, only write, — to Jemmy
" Longſhanks or bearer, that will be
" ſufficient.—Sir, I thank you, I hope we
" ſhall have better ſucceſs another time.
" I hope ſo too, Mr. Longſhanks ; good
" day to you. Sir, your very humble
" ſervant."

" You may add, if you pleaſe, Cap-
" tain-General of the band of Gentlemen
" STOCK-BROKERS.—

This example may be multiplied to a
thouſand ; but as the neceſſary explanation
of it has taken up more room than I ima-
gined, I ſhall wave giving any further
inſtances of the ſame kind, and ſhall leave
the judicious reader to form a caſe *e con-
tra*, wherein a trader ſells, for the reſcounters,

counters, and wants to lower the price, in order to buy in, under what he has agreed to deliver at; and to follow this man to the Coffee-houfe, where he will be found exclaiming againft the meafures of the miniftry, and pronouncing the nation to be on the brink of ruin. And in the room of other examples, I fhall here introduce fome remarks, which I hope the public will think deferving of the moft ferious attention.

Granting then, that any tradefman of this great metropolis has acted fuch a fcene as I have juft defcribed, can it be fuppofed that he will fit down quietly with his lofs ? a lofs—which the profits of his trade will not, perhaps, recover in many years. No, certainly, he will fport again, and probably a fecond lofs may lead the way to bankruptcy; or grant that he gains, it is all upon honor; and perhaps when the day comes that he is to receive a great balance in his favour,

which

which would indemnify him for his former loffes, his Broker turns out a LAME
DUCK*; by which, he has the mor-
tification of lofing this balance without
refource, and probably of feeing his Broker re-eftablifhed at Jonathan's, for a paltry compofition to his creditors within
the houfe, while he himfelf is declared a
Bankrupt, for his inability to pay his lawful creditors their juft demands; which
inability has arofe from his having too
punctually paid his debts of honor, to
the honorable gentleman, who has now
left him to fhift for himfelf : but the
worft of all is, that, confcious of his own
folly, he has never placed this great lofs
to account, and his books being regu-
larly kept, except in this particular, it

* A name given in 'Change-Alley to thofe who
refufe to fulfil their contracts. There are fome of
thefe at almoft every refcounters. The punifhment
for non-payment is banifhment from Jonathan's, but
they can ftill act as Brokers at the offices.

appears

appears upon the examination under the
commiffion, that a large fum has been
received in a fhort fpace of time, and
no account is given how it is expend-
ed; this naturally leads to an enquiry
of the Bankrupt, what is become of
this money? To which he will perhaps anfwer, (if he is a man that is not
paft the time of life for the indulgence of
fenfual pleafure) that he has fpent it in
high living, and on women; for the laft
of vices that a man of fpirit would chufe
to own, is gaming, as it carries with it
no excufe, having no gratification to
plead; and is befides the moft blame-
able of any in a tradefman. This account
not proving fatisfactory, he is condemned
for the fuppofed fins of his youth, but in
reality for his follies in the Alley, to a
perpetual imprifonment.

If an inftance of this kind happens
only once in five or fix years, is it not
enough to make a humane people lament
that

that such a gaming scheme subsists in the
very heart of the city ? ought it not to
silence all clamors, as well as all lam-
poons and satires on card playing at the
court-end of the town ? for how trifling
are the sums generally played for at cards,
in comparison of the deep stakes in the
Alley ? how infinitely do the consequences fall short of those, which attend
gaming in the funds ? In one case, noble-
men and gentry dip their estates, and
impoverish their families; in the other,
substantial merchants and citizens, who
are the very soul of commerce, are
ruined; and the state, that subsists by
the extent and flourishing condition of its
commercial interest, must suffer in the
end.

Again, let it be considered, that in
some at least, of our grand card assem-
blies, all foul play is excluded; and the
chances are equal, except where superior
skill in the game gives the advantage.
Now

Now no fuperior fkill in any game at
cards can give an advantage equal to that
which, the crafts and fubtilties practifed
by the old ftandards in the Alley gives
them, over the young and unexperienced;
and this fhould not only deter men from
engaging on fuch unequal terms, but
fhould likewife induce them to be very
fparing of their reflections on thofe who
have loft a confiderable fum in the Alley,
and have quietly fat down with the lofs;
fince fuch perfons might be ignorant at
firft, that the practice of STOCK-JOBBING
was difhoneft in itfelf; or that in order to
fucceed in it, a man muft diveft himfelf
of every fentiment of humanity and inte-
grity, and muft be deaf to the cries of the
wretched whom his fuccefs has reduced
to mifery: he therefore, who, having
found his error, fubmits to the fatal
blow, and tamely wears the name of dupe,
rather than ftay in the Alley till he becomes a fharper, merits the compaffion,
and were it not my own cafe, I had faid,
the

the applaufe of a chriftian people.   A
French author very juftly fays :

Le défir de gagner, qui nuit & jour occupe,
  Eft un dangereux aiguillon.
Souvent quoique l'efprit, quoique le cœur foit bon,
  On commence par etre dupe
  On finit par étre fripon.

Happy therefore is that man, who has
only the folly of being a dupe to reflec-
tion ; and not the infamy of ftaying in the
Alley, 'till he was a fripon, or fharper.
In a word, the chance of gaining is very
fmall, and the uncertainty of being paid
when you have gained very great ; for
which reafon, I intreat thofe who have
not yet entered the Alley, never to frequent it on a jobbing account ; and thofe
who have finned already, to go their ways
and fin no more, left a worfe thing
come unto them, left their fortunes and
their liberty, fall a facrifice to the fatal
confequences of repeated loffes in the
                              Alley,

Alley, and their names, which once ſtood foremoſt in the bright records of unſullied honor, ſhould be funk into oblivion, or by the haſty judgment of an uncharitable world, be branded with undeſerved infamy.   For how few are there in our days, who entertain the ſentiments of a late noble author, " convinced as I " am," ſays he, " that every man has " his failings, and that few are exempt " from malice, I ſhall never be ready to " confirm a report to the prejudice of " my neighbour's honor ; for if he " proves guilty, I ſhall be ſorry to in- " creaſe the burden of his crime by my " reflections, and if he is found to be " innocent, I ſhall be charmed to think " that I was not of the number of his " calumniators."

I ſhall now give an account of the tranſactions of the profeſſors themſelves,
who

who, like the members of other colleges, have different degrees, according to the extent of their genius, or the length of time they have belonged to the fociety. At J————'s there are SERVITORS, NO-VICES, PUPILS, TUTORS, and DOCTORS; the latter of which, are eafily known by their pride and arrogance, which breaks forth upon every occafion, into declamations againft the frefh-men or NOVICES; and in praife of their own fuperior fkill and dignity.—If any of my readers have ever employed a DOCTOR in the art, they will eafily recollect fome fuch advertifements of his fkill, as this—" I am always " to be found in the very worft times, " and know how things ftand, and the " trim of the houfe better than thefe " young boys, that live but a few days " in the Alley, and then are heard no " more of:" which means no more, than that they can fhave clofer, than the young ones—which may be taken either

in

in a literal, or a figurative fenfe*. Tu-
TORS are thofe who take NOVICES for
their PUPILS, and finding their ignorance
(owing to their innocence,) make bargains with them, and bring them into
credit with the houfe, in which they fuffer them to go alone, as foon as they
have tricked them out of half their fortunes, for teaching them an art, which
if they have any honefty left, they quit
as foon as they know the infamy of it,
leaving their tutors to enjoy the fruits of
their guilty inftructions—the tutorfhip at
J——'s has generally been in the hands
of Jews, and with great propriety one

---

* The reader will remember that in the preface I
obferved, that the affembly at J——'s, is com-
pofed of men of all forts of mechanic trades, which
they have quitted for the lucrative, but difhoneft
employment of Stock Jobbing : among the reft, one
worthy perfonage has raifed himfelf from what the
vulgar call, a penny barber, to the degree of a Doctor, with the addition of a genteel equipage, and
an elegant country manfion.

Aaron,

Aaron, was for many years high prieft.
SERVITORS are thofe who wait on their
mafters commands, and are ready to
do all the dirty bufinefs they order
them; and which they do not care
to appear in themfelves; fuch as affert-
ing, that Stocks were done at a different
price than they really were, at any particular hour—or buying and felling under hand for their mafters, a large quantity of any of the funds for the refcounters, in order to raife or fall the STOCKS
at pleafure, which bufinefs they tranfact
with a brother SERVITOR, who is in the
plot; and after the end is obtained, for
which thefe bargains were made, they
are cancelled, and the bounty of the
mafter is equally divided, which by
the bye, is but very fmall; and therefore the SERVITORS are to be diftinguifhed by their fhabby appearance, and
their frequenting the door of J——'s,
which they can but feldom afford to
en-

enter*. I remember indeed one excep-
tion, which was of a favorite Servitor
who was one morning employed to tranfact fuch part of a great man's bufinefs,
as he himfelf could not perform for want
of time ; and his allowance for this over-
plus of the other's bufinefs, amounted to
15 *l.* fterling; by this it appears that
jobbing muft be the principal fupport of,
and what enriches the gentlemen of the
Alley, for it is next to incredible that any
Broker, (who was only moderately fond
of wealth) fhould really transfer in one
morning, betwixt the hours of 9 and 12,
fo much Stocks, or Annuities, (for
which he has no more than 2 *s.* 6 *d. per
Cent.*) as would enable him to fpare his

---

* Every perfon who enters Jonathan's to do any
bufinefs there, pays 6d. at the bar, for which he is
intitled to firing, pen, ink, and paper, and a fmall
cup of chocolate ; and if he underftands the bufinefs,
is as good a Broker for that day (at leaft for his own
affairs) as the beft.

Ser-

SERVITOR 15 *l.* but when once a JOB-
BING account enters the lifts, as there are
no bounds to this fort of gaming, it is
not to be wondered at, if on a fettling-
day, after any refcounters, a DOCTOR of
the Alley fhould be obliged to take a
SERVITOR at the rate of 20 *l. per diem** ;
another part of the SERVITOR's bufinefs
is, to make and carry paragraphs of falfe
intelligence to the printers of the public
papers, whom we often find confeffing
that they were impofed upon in particular
articles of news ; and it were to be wifhed
that this apology was always true, and

---

* Since the publication of the firft edition of this
work, a gentleman has communicated to the author
the following anecdote—That there is an office not
far from the Exchange, kept by two brokers, whofe
commiffions for three months paft, have amounted
upon a moderate calculation to £ 100, one day with
another ; and fo pofitive is he in his computation,
that he adds, he would willingly have rented the profits of their office, at that fum, every day fince the
firft report of a congrefs.

E   that

that the public might have no room to suppose that for 5 s. they insert any piece of intelligence, without considering the consequences.

The gentlemen of the Alley have like-wise their TERMS and VACATIONS, but there are no stated times for these in general, though in time of war, we may fix the commencement of their principal Term, to the beginning of November; and its duration to the end of January following.

In this term, there are several sorts of business to transact which keep the Alley in a perpetual ferment, without the least relaxation; insomuch that even many of the DOCTORS, are obliged to lay up their equipages, and others to send their high bred hunters to the livery stables. TERM generally begins a few days before the drawing of the lottery, when those who have contracted to take, or are

already

already poffeffed of, more tickets than
they can poffibly hold, (in the language
of 'Change Alley, begin to open the bud-
get, or to let the cat out of the bag)
and thefe may not improperly be ftiled
the Bulls, Plaintiffs ;—and the oppofite party, who have agreed to deliver a
quantity of tickets without being poffeffed
of them, the Bears, Defendants.
The caufe is depending nine months before it comes to a final decifion ; there
are indeed little trials of fkill betwixt the
Bulls and Bears at the end of every
month, from February to November,
becaufe for each of thefe months there are
contracts made, for twenty times as many
tickets, as there are in the whole lottery ;
but the grand and final decifion is on
Friday before the firft day of drawing,
when that is appointed by the Lottery
Act to be on any Monday ; but when it
is ordered to commence further on in
the week, then the day of fettling at
J——'s is altered, fo as to make the fet-

tling

tling accompts happen a day or two at moſt, before the drawing begins.

It would be tedious, and indeed in ſome meaſure needleſs to give more examples than one, of the chicanery practiſed by the profeſſors of the college, and of the various artifices they make uſe of to impoſe on each other, and the public in general, becauſe the ſame meaſures muſt be purſued ; and the ſame tricks played for all JOBBING accounts, in every different branch of the funds ; for which reaſon I ſhall confine myſelf, to a jobbing account in the Lottery, as being that which affects a larger body of the public than any other ; for there are numbers who annually adventure in Lottries who know nothing of the other funds ; and probably have no property in them.

As a proſe writer, and only a bare narrator of facts, I cannot properly call in the aſſiſtance of the fairy train, nor yet conjure
up

up aerial fpirits to convey my readers
through the jarring elements to the place,
where, for my own convenience, I would
have them tranfported; I fhall therefore
only fimply intreat them to awake the
powers of their imaginations, and by
their ftrength fuppofe themfelves convey-
ed to the famous college of jobbers, not
inferior to any college of jefuits; where
I muft leave them to recollect, and call
up the idea of Bartholomew Fair, or
fome country wake, that they may have
a juft refemblance of that horrid din of
confufed voices; and that motly appearance of various characters which prefent
themfelves to their view, at their entrance
into the college—while I for a moment
paufe—to confider in what language and
form, I fhall explain the fubjects of their
wild uproar.

Shall I throw it into dialogue ? No,
'tis impracticable; for it confifts of fuch
a medley of news, quarrels, prices of dif-

E 3   ferent

ferent funds, calling of names, adjufting
of accounts, &c. &c. continually circu-
lating in an intermixed chaos of confu-
fion, that it will not admit of digefting
into that pure decent method of exprefing
a familiar converfation.

Shall I invoke the comic mufe; and
in her lively vein of humour expofe the
deformity of thefe fons of iniquity? No,
the characters are too low, the fubject
too mean, and the plots too dirty, unlefs
I was writing for a ftrolling company;
and the piece were to be reprefented at a
booth on a common, in the wilds of
Kent.

Since then no borrowed ftyle will fuit
it, nor no characters aptly reprefent it,
let me give the explanation in their own
language; and only inform fuch of my
readers as are not likely ever to fee
J——'s in reality, that their nonfenfi-
cal medley of difcourfe neareft refembles
the advertifements of the late famous ora-

tor

tor Henley, a fpecimen of which I have
procured, that the public may judge for
themfelves.*

The grand fcene opens a little after
twelve at noon, (at which time the tranf-

*Jan 30, 1756. K. Charles I's Charge to Hen-
ly's Jury! At the Oratory K. GEORGE's Chapel.
Sunday—N. B. Laft Lord's day, two or three
puzzlepates faid—I had too much Divinity, on the
Thomas's and John's—was too grave—BrethrenPref-
byterians fay—Religion is a grave Thing; and I
am not grave enough: Split the difference, but don't
fplit me; Bleffed K. Charles I. in the Common
Prayer-Book; Ora pro nobis! And for thy Grand
Nephew K. George! And my Reafons! Loyal to
the Hilts! And God's Providences and Man's
Duties,—I hope, that is grave,—the Bible is wife and
merry,--whether Chrift was for fafting or againft it.
Louis's Challenge and St J's's Anfwer—Genl.
Johnfon refign'd—Pr. Naffau's heart!—Mr. Whit-
field's Victory—The Art of Starving, and the Bright-
eft fhort Stripes, all for the Good of the People, who,
therefore will be for me, and I'll beat their Impoveri-
fhers—after that the beft in the Houfe—10062—
Henley! be boldeft in the Land of Reafon—
and Speech on Speech—difpatch thy Foes—Blood
for Blood.

fer

fer books of moſt of the offices are ſhut
for the day) and generally the actors hold
forth in the following manner, and almoſt all at once: ' Tickets—Tickets—
' South Sea Stock for the opening—
' Navy-Bills—Bank Stock for the reſ-
' counters—Long Annuities (*here the*
' *waiter calls*) Chance—Chance—Chance,
' *Mr. Chance is not here, Sir, he is over*
' *at is Office*—Here Tickets for Au-
' guſt—Omnium gatherum for Septem-
' ber—Scrip for the third payment—
' 3 per cent. conſolidated, gentlemen
' —Here Mr. Full (*whiſpers a friend,*
' *but is overheard*) they are all BULLS by
' G—d, but I'll be d—d if they have
' any of my Stock, I'll go to Bath, and
' not come near them till the reſcoun-
' ters—Here Bank Circulation, who
' buys Bank Circulation—Tickets for
' the drawing, gentlemen—Well, what
' have you to do in Tickets for the draw-
' ing, Mr. Mulberry. I am a ſeller of
' five hundred, Sir—and I am a Buyer,
Sir

' Sir, but pray at what price?—Why, as
' you are a friend, Mr. Point-royal, I
' shall give you the turn, you shall have
' them at 14. ‡ The turn Mr. Mulber-
' ry, why, do you think I do not know
' what I am about? they are all sellers
' at 13—Well then, you shall have them
' at 13—I will take them at 12, and no
' otherwise—Well, you shall have them,
' put 'em down (for the drawing mind)
' but, d—n it, Tom, where did you
' get that paste wig? Why, you son of
' a b—h, it is as good as your mop.—
' India Stock without the dividend.
' Have you any thing to do in India
' Stock, Monsieur-sham it? Non pas,
' Monsieur, bien obligé, Shaw—I have
' been talking French so long to Sir
' Harry Travelsick, that I forget my-

‡ This means 10 *l.* or 11 *l.* 14*s.* as the price is, but
this short method has been invented to save the gen-
tlemens breath, otherwise it would be impossible for
their lungs to hold out.

' felf— I have nothing to do, Sir, I am
' but juft come from Tunbridge, (an-
' grily) India bonds, who buys India
' bonds—no buyers in the market. Well,
' Mr. Backward, where fhall we dine to-
' day ? — You have never a pig in ftore,
' have you? No, no, Mr. Sharpfet,
' thefe are bad times, I have made no-
' thing of it this term yet; but hufh,
' don't talk of pig, for here comes the
' proud Dr. Low-pifs, who never looks
' pleafant at the beft; and fhould you
' mention Swine's flefh in his hearing,
' we fhall make him as furly as Old
' Nick.*—Enter Kit Cot—and Mr.

---

* In the famous South-Sea year, a haunch of ve-
nifon fold for five guineas, which was a proof of the
luxury of the jobbers of that æra.

Mr. Backward is an inftance of luxury in another
kind; he is fond of a pig prepared for his table in
the following manner—it muft be taken from the
fow foon after it is littered, and laid on a foft cufhion
by the fire fide, where it muft be fed with Naples
bifcuits and cream, 'till it is a fortnight old, and
then be whipped to death and roafted.

Ver-

‘ Verjuice, from Spring-gardens, with
‘ each a book in his hand—Here, EVERY
‘ MAN HIS OWN BROKER, I am a feller
‘ for money—and I am a feller for time—
‘ to them Mr. Skin’it, formerly a butcher,
‘ Mr. Onion, Sam. Dangerlefs, Joe Dirty-
‘ face, the baker, and Tom Steel the com-
‘ mon-council-man, who all at once de-
‘ mand, what is it? Any new fubfcription,
‘ Mr. Verjuice; I buy, I buy,—no, no,
‘ Gentlemen, it is not fo good a thing, it is
‘ a d—’d impudent libel, againft all the
‘ members of this facred college; and I
‘ would give all Spring-gardens to fee the
‘ author well punifhed for his infolence;
‘ here he gives directions how to buy and
‘ fell Stock; and lays open the whole of
‘ our tranfactions; and all forfooth be-
‘ caufe he has loft his money amongft us.
‘ — Thoufands have fhared the fame fate,
‘ why fhould he make fuch a noife about
‘ it, or why injure all to be revenged on
‘ a few; ’twas neither you nor I that
                                    ftripp’d

' ftripp'd him, 'twas Aaron the Jew,
' Bob Falftaff, and old Hodge, and two
' or three more—Well, pray don't be in
' a paffion, gentlemen ; pray what are you
' going to do with the books ? do, why
' fell them at a low price, you know that's
' the only way ; and then tell all our
' friends out of doors, what curfed ftuff
' it is ; and that it was done here at—how
' much Mr. Skin'it ? why I will give you
' ten pence money—(both) you fhall have
' them—*calls out*, done at ten pence, gen-
' tlemen—pray get it put in Chance's
' lift, 'twill damn the book effectually*—
' Here, who'll fell a hundred for time—
' *Sam Dangerlefs replies*, I am a feller of a

---

* Saturday May 30, 1761.--- Mr. Chance is a very
worthy good natured man, who is arrived at the
higheft pinacle of fame, for diftributing the favors
of fortune, like his miftrefs, at hazard, fometimes
giving 10,000 l. to Blockheads, and to men of the
greateft merit, a Blank. Unluckily for the gentleman in queftion, he has not put the Alley price, of
Every Man his own Broker, in any of his lifts.

' hun-

' hundred for time—you ſhall have them
' at nine pence for September next—I will
' take them at eight pence—you ſhall
' have them—done at eight pence, gentle-
' men, for September—a good bargain, I
' ſhall get them at the ſtalls for a penny,
' long before that time.—Tom Steel now
' interpoſes, and makes as formal an ha-
' rangue as if he were pleading in the city
' parliament for ſome darling privilege.—
' Gentlemen, you are highly in the wrong
' to take ſo much notice of this paltry
' performance, or its author ; truſt me,
' the beſt thing you can do is to let him
' alone, the thing will die of itſelf ; be-
' ſides, he really can do us no harm, for
' we are ſo ſtrong a body, that he may as
' well attempt to beat down the monu-
' ment with an OLD SHOE-HORN, as to de-
' ſtroy our college ; we are too well ſup-
' ported, leave him to me, paſs quietly
' by him in the ſtreets, and do not ſtare
' at him as if you ſaw a monſter, for that
only

' only marks rage, and a confeffion of
' guilt:—I have a fafer and more quiet
' way, it is but arming our knights, and
' baronets in our caufe, and this moth will
' foon be crufh'd. I can add no more,
' for here are fome ftrangers coming in,
' therefore let's adjourn the fubject,—
' but by the by, (*whifpers*) I have voted
' for a filk gown to day, I hate to be
' number'd among the common livery—
' Here old annuities without the divi-
' dend—Enter Mynheer Vanderdouble-
' face (with a packet of letters)—two
' mails from Holland and three from
' Flanders. Ik fal never go thro' myn
' bufinefs, 'tis too much; (looking round
' him wat has my news fent all de
' dgentlemen to de poft-huis—well—that
' is ongeluckt, for ik muft buy een groot
' deal of ftock, dar is heel good news—
' de Eelle-ifle is taken."——

Having thus given a fpecimen of the
daily tumult at J——'s, I am to apolo-
gize

gize for letting any thing fo very low appear in print, by affuring the public, that nothing could have induced me to have given it a place, but the defire of fhewing them what a trifling fet of people they are in fubjection to; for I call it fubjection, when fo large a body of people, as that part of the public who have concerns in the funds are, tamely fubmit to think, fpeak, and act, upon the judgments of thefe gentry.

I fhall now return to Mr. Point-royal, and juft exhibit a leaf or two of his jobbing book, before I take my leave of him.

Page 17, Lottery Tickets for the Drawing.

Bought, *viz.* - - to take	Sold - - - to deliver
200 of Levy - - 10 *l.* 15 *s.*	600 to Mr. Buck a 10 *l.* 5 *s.*
100 of Benjamin - - 12 *s.*	300 to Mr. Skin flint -- 8 *s.*
100 of Solomon - - - 14 *s.*	200 to Dr. Wool - - 10 *s.*
100 of Reuben - - - 18 *s.*	400 to Aaron Avarice 11 *s.*
500 Mr. Mulbery. - - 15 *s.*	
────	────
1000	1500

It

It appears by this account that Mr. Point-royal is a BEAR for 500 Tickets; that is, he has fold 500 more than he has bought, and confequently he wifhes they may fall; and as a means to bring it about, he runs up and down the houfe, a few days before the drawing, declaring, that the tickets do not go off, that he has paffed by all the offices, and did not fee one cuftomer in any of them; and in fhort, that the price muft come down. The reafon of this conduct is obvious. Tickets at the time of his acting thus, are confiderably above the price he has agreed to deliver at; and fhould they continue fo 'till the drawing, he will be obliged to buy 500 to adjuft his account at a much higher price than he has fold at. This is only one account, and that a fmall one; but let us fuppofe the accounts of the greateft part of the houfe to ftand thus, and that the majority are BEARS; it is upon the difcovery of this,

this, that the debates in the cause begin
to grow warm, and the counsel to rail at
each other, and brow-beat the evidence—
This produces a scene of amazing confu-
sion and uproar; and the public are
obliged to give that price for Tickets, in
the offices, which the sentence passed in the
college fixes on them: thus, for instance,
If the BULLS get the better of the con-
test, by holding their Tickets to the last,
and oblige the BEARS to buy on their
own terms, then the price of Tickets
rises considerably, not from their intrinsic value, but from the artificial scarcity
in the Alley: but if, on the contrary, the
BEARS gain the victory by a seeming in-
difference, and by raising a thousand artful stories, which frighten the BULLS,
and cause them to sell all at once, then
the price falls, from the market's being
overstocked, and the public will thereby
procure them at a low price. I would
therefore advise all private adventurers
either to buy very soon after the first
coming

coming out of the Tickets, which generally is in June, or July, or elfe to wait
'till the very morning of drawing, and
buy, an hour or two, before the wheel
goes round.

It would puzzle my readers to divine
the method of fettling or adjufting (as
they call it) fuch an account as Mr.
Point-royal's, and if I were not to give a
flight fketch of the manner of doing it,
it would be thought incredible that it
fhould ever enter into the heads of any
fet of men, to invent fuch a perplexed
and intricate form, of adjufting an account.

For the fake of brevity, and to render
myfelf as intelligible as poffible, I fhall
take only one article on each fide of Mr.
Point-royal's account.   Againft the day
of fettling he has made out, what he calls
his lift, with which he appears in court,
and once more accofts Mr. Mulberry—
                                        Sir,

Sir, I am to take 500 Tickets of you, do you deliver them? No, Sir.—Who have you got then? Let me fee—I have got Mr. Sham-it, go to him for 400, and fee if you can adjuft that, while I fee who I have got for the other 100—*(goes on)* I am put to you Mr. Sham-it, by Mr. Mulberry, for 400 Tickets. Well, Sir, you muft go to Dangerlefs *(goes on)* Mr. Dangerlefs, can you deliver me 400 Tickets for Mr. Sham-it? Yes, Sir, are you ready to take them? No, Sir, I am to deliver to Aaron Avarice—*(calls)* Aaron Avarice here, will you take your 400 Tickets of Mr. Dangerlefs? No, Sir, I give you James the fon of Zebedee.— Zounds, Sir, that won't do, he is Mr. Mulberry's partner; and I am to take of him—Well then, let me fee, oh! deliver them to Mr. Town-ditch,—aye, aye, take 'em to Town-ditch, and there they'll fettle.

In fhort, Mr. Town-ditch agrees to take 'em, being in want of 400 for a
cuftomer

cuftomer (for he is no jobber, but when obliged to act for a principal) but here another difficulty arifes, about the price they are to be done at; Mr. Town-ditch is to pay for them, and will take them at no other price, than that which he agreed for with Aaron Avarice; which happens to be a great deal lower than Mr. Danger-lefs fold them at to Mr. Sham-it; at laft however, Mr. Town-ditch being a good natured man, (and knowing Mr. Sham-it to be a DOCTOR, who has never been a LAME DUCK) agrees to pay for them at 12 s. to fatisfy Mr. Dangerlefs, who al-ways takes care to be on the fure fide.*

Thus we have adjufted 400 of Mr. Point-royal's tickets; and happy will it be, if he fettles any more fo eafily; for fometimes thefe gentlemen put one an-other about from man to man, 'till they

---

* Dangerlefs is fo lame a Duck, that he has broke both legs three or f ur times; but by the help of good fplintering, is at laft perfectly reftored.

have

have gone all round the houfe.—The
method of entering thefe accompts when
adjufted, is to the full as abfurd ; and
would afford no entertainment or inftruction, for which reafon only I omit it. The
remainder of this term is employed in
buying and felling of Tickets during the
drawing ; and in infuring them on divers
conditions.

In order to have a clear idea of the
defign of infuring Tickets, it is neceffary
to obferve, that not above one half
of the Tickets in any Lottery are fairly
fold out to the public before the drawing;
by fairly fold out, I mean, fo as not to
come to market again; for a great many
people buy a quantity of Tickets, without
any intention of venturing a fingle fhilling in the Lottery.   Thefe buy at a low
price, and when they find an opportunity
of felling to advantage, they bring them
to market again; and if this opportunity does not offer, before the drawing
begins,

begins, they generally infure them; for which purpofe there are a fet of MASTERS of ARTS, and DOCTORS, who open offices in J——'s, and pafte up their names over their feveral Stalls nearly in this manner. Tickets infured from Blanks by Dr. Squintum* and Co. Their principal bufinefs is to infure Tickets from blanks, or in other words, to give an undrawn Ticket, for every one that is drawn a blank, during the time they are infured. This branch of infuring, is calculated to ferve thofe who go into the wheel with a number of Tickets, defigning to fell them at a high price, if they grow fcarce, or the great prizes happen to ftay long in the wheel : but whether the infuring tickets in this cafe,

---

* Note, This gentleman is a diftant relation to the famous Dr. Squintum, who infures old women and children from damnation, at his offices at Tottenham-court and Moorfields—they have both been admired in the open air; but are now happily fettled within doors.

or

or the rifking the chance of the wheel,
and buying frefh tickets in the room of
thofe drawn blanks, with the money
that is faved by not infuring, be moft
advantageous, is matter of doubt; for
the DOCTORS in the alley, like moft
Doctors out of it, differ in opinion; fome
infuring, and others running the chance
of the Wheel.

The price of infurance from blanks,
is generally from 5 s. to 5 l. as the drawing advances; and it fets off at firft,
lower, or higher, in proportion to the
number of blanks there are to a prize in
the fcheme of the Lottery: thus, for
inftance, the price of infurance from
blanks, in the prefent Lottery, will be
cheaper than in the laft, becaufe there
are fewer blanks to a prize; and confequently the infurer runs lefs hazard.

Hitherto we have only treated of infurance of real property, we are now to
exhibit

exhibit the sporting part of insurance, which is almost as considerable as the other; and is on the whole much more profitable.

As the gentlemen Insurers, previous to their opening their books, have held a committee, in which the nicest calculations have been made, and the price fixed, with the moderate allowance to themselves of 25 *per Cent.* profit upon the whole, it matters not to them, whether the persons who bring a list of numbers to insure, are really possessed of those tickets or not, provided they comply with the conditions required of those, who are possessed of Tickets, *viz.* to deliver up the blanks when drawn, in exchange for undrawn Tickets. I am therefore at liberty to carry any indifferent number, or the number of my Ticket, (if I have one) the only difference is this, that, in the one case, I give up the blank
for

for an undrawn Ticket; and in the other, I allow the value of the blank, and take either an undrawn Ticket, or, (if I am no adventurer in the lottery) the value of an undrawn, in money.

Another method of sporting is, to insure for prizes, that is, to give in, any list of numbers whatever; and if any of them are drawn prizes, during the time they are insured, I receive for every prize so drawn, the value of a twenty pounds prize, in money. The price of insuring in this manner, is generally from 1 s. 6 d. (the first day) to 5 s. towards the end of the drawing *.

Having

*There is hardly a 'prentice boy, or a waiter to a tavern, or coffee-house, in the neighbourhood of the Alley, that is not a sporter, in the two last-mentioned kinds of insurance. — Some years ago there was a method practised in the Alley of letting out Tickets for a day, or any part of a day, during the drawing, and if they came up prizes in the time they were let out, they belonged to the hirer,

who

Having thus given an account of the
bufinefs tranfacted at the beginning of
term, I fhall only obferve, that all is
pretty quiet after the drawing of the Lottery is over, 'till towards the end of Term,
when the raifing of the fupplies for the
fervice of the new year, throws the whole
houfe into a frefh ferment; but for an account of this, I muft refer my readers to
chap. 4. and fhall conclude this, with relating their manner of fpending the vacations.
The fpring vacation generally begins in
March, when fuch of the gentlemen of
the Alley as are in town, pafs their time

who was generally faid to be riding a horfe in
'Change Alley, to which the race-horfes, mentioned
in the Preface alludes--Quære--Is not the giving in a
lift of undrawn numbers, taken at random out of a
Lottery-book, and infuring them for prizes as above,
the fame thing, as hiring of horfes was formerly?
If fo, how juft the motto in the title page,

Quid faciunt leges ubi fola pecunia regnat?

Of what ufe are laws, where money governs all?

at

at J——'s in buying and felling of green peas, mackrel, &c. by way of piddling, to keep their hands in at jobbing, 'till Term comes on again.

The method of playing at this game is, to buy or fell 100 pecks of green peas for the earliest feafon, or first coming in at a particular high price; and the way of adjusting the account is, to fend to Shuttleworth's to know the price of the first peck of peas that were brought to market; according to which the buyer, or feller, at J——'s regulates his account, and pays, or receives, the difference betwixt the price they were done at by him and his antagonist, and the price at market. The mackrel bargains are generally for 1000, at their first coming in, and are adjusted much in the fame manner; for as foon as they are cried about the streets, the contending parties buy as many as they want for a dinner; and this fettles their accounts, and

F 2   furnifhes

furnifhes them with a delicate repaft.
Now as thefe gentlemen follow only their
own weak judgments, or the price of the
precedent year in this fport, I fhould
think an underftanding gardener, and
a fkilful fifhmonger, might have the beft
of the game; for the one might give a
better guefs by obferving the backward-
nefs or forwardnefs of the fpring, and the
other by knowing the run of the market
at Billingfgate.

Another manner of fpending the vacations is, in infuring on the lives of fuch
unfortunate gentlemen, as may happen
to ftand accountable to their country for
mifconduct. I am not willing to difturb
the afhes of the peaceful dead, or I could
give an inftance of this cruel paftime, the
parallel of which, is not to be met with,
in the hiftory of any civilized nation: but
I hope we fhall hear no more of fuch
deteftable gaming; and therefore as a
fcene of this kind fully laid open, might
aftonifh,

aftonifh, but could not convey inftruction, humanity bids me draw the veil, and not render any fet of men unneceffarily odious.

Infuring of property in any city or town that is befieged, is a common branch of bufinefs ; out ingenious gamefters, ever ftudious to invent new, and variegate old games, have, out of this lawful game, (for infurance in general is no more than a game at chances) contrived a new amufement for the gentlemen of the Alley ; which is for one perfon to give another 40 *l.* and in cafe Pondicherry (for in-ftance) is taken from the French by a particular time, the perfon to whom the 40 *l.* is paid, is to repay 100 *l.* but if, on the contrary, the fiege is raifed before the time mentioned, he keeps the 40 *l.* In proportion as the danger the place is in of being taken increafes, the premium of infurance advances ; and when the place has been fo fituated, that repeated

F 3　　　　intel-

intelligence could be received of the progrefs of the fiege, I have known the infurance rife to 90 *l.* for 100 *l.* A fine
field this opens for fpreading falfe reports,
and making private letters from the
Hague, *&c!* ——— but how infinitely
more harmlefs to trifle with property,
than to affect the life of a fellow fubject,
or to injure him with the public, to ferve
a private end!

I cannot more properly clofe this chapter, than by leaving upon the minds of
my readers this felf-evident inference from
the whole.

That it is almoft impoffible for any
Broker, who is a jobber, (and there are
but few that are not) to give candid
impartial advice when to buy into, or
fell out of, the public funds.

C H A P.

C H A P. III.

Of the method of Transferring and Accepting,
or of Buying into, and Selling out of, the
Public Funds, giving full directions how to
transact this business without the assistance
of a Broker.—Form of Receipts given on
transferring Stock. — Explanation of the
meaning of $\frac{1}{8}$, $\frac{3}{8}$, $\frac{5}{8}$, $\frac{7}{8}$, being part of the prices
annexed to the lists of the funds printed in the
news-papers, chiefly designed for the use of
those who live in the country.—A short method of casting up any odd quantity of Stock,
at the price of the same per cent.—Laws in
force to oblige the clerks of the Bank, and
other public offices, to aid and assist all manner of persons whatever to transfer their property in the several Funds.—Penalty on refusal,
—Laws in force relative to Brokers.—Advice
concerning Draughts on Bankers—and Letters of Attorney.—Table shewing the days
and hours of transferring at the several public
offices, and the amount of the several capital

Stocks

Stocks, and Annuities; to which is added, A Lift of the Holidays obferved at the faid Offices.

THERE are numberlefs tranf- actions in the common courfe of bufinefs, which are in them- felves extremely eafy to perform; but which fome through ignorance, others through prejudice, and many more for want of refolution, commit to the care of others; and affign them a falary, which often they can but badly fpare, for the execution of that, which with a little in- duftry and attention, they may be mafters of themfelves in a few days.

Of this number, is the bufinefs now under our confideration, which by the force of cuftom has been configned to the management of a fet of men, who were unknown to fociety 'till within the laft half century; and who, by way of grati- tude, very fairly attempted in the year

1720,

1720, to turn their masters out of doors, or in other words, who, not content with their poor allowance of 2s. 6d. for brokerage, laid a plan for apropriating to themselves the whole fortunes of their benefactors, in which, for a short time, they succeeded to a miracle; and have ever since been piddling with the public property, and enriching themselves at the expence of the innocent and unwary.

Let it then be every man's care, who has any property in the funds, to prevent the increase of the power, and influence, as well as of the number, of these invaders of their property, by boldly and manfully resolving to transact his own business. Do you want to buy? examine first the funds and their prices in the daily papers, or if it suits you better, search the lists already mentioned in Chap. I. and when you have determined what fund to buy into, concerning the choice of which,

you

you have likewise my opinion in the same
chapter, go boldly to the office where
the fund you have made choice of is
transferred, and be not difmayed at the
wild uproar, and confufed noife which
will at firſt ſtrike your aſtoniſhed fenſes—
many of you have ſupported more for
your amuſement, on the firſt night of a
new play; and others, at the nocturnal re-
vels of the choice ſpirits; and will you not
now do it, to redeem the management of
public property, from the hands of pro-
feſſed ſharpers; and to refcue the beſt of
governments from a ſlaviſh dependence on
theſe ſons of rapine, for every million extraordinary that it ſtands in need of, in
time of war?

Advance then, and attend a few mi-
nutes to the confuſed cries that refound
from all quarters; and you will foon
find what you want—a feller of the
fum you propoſe to buy; you have only
to demand the price, which if there has
been

been no particular news to occasion a sud-
den variation, you will find by comparing
it, to be nearly the same with that of the
preceding day; if he is a common seller,
he will name you the whole price as $74\frac{3}{8}$
or whatever it happens to be; but if he is
a DOCTOR, or MASTER of ARTS in the
Alley, he will only tell you the fraction of
the price, *viz.* $\frac{1}{8}$ or $\frac{5}{8}$, and if he finds you
do not know the principal sum, he will
thereby be assured that you are not a
Broker, and will probably quit you in
search of one, for his interest is, to deal
with none but Brokers; as your's is, to
do your business without them, therefore
let him go, you will soon be accosted by
some other seller, who, perhaps, is not a
Broker, for there are plenty of such every
transfer-day; and it is your business by
adding one, to increase the number.—
Should you wait a little, and no person
offers to sell to you, venture to exert
yourself, and call out lustily, that you
are a Buyer of the sum you want, what

ever

ever it be,—truſt me, you will find very
little difference betwixt the articulation of
the few words requiſite upon this occaſion,
and the common aſpiration you are ſometimes forced to make uſe of, in calling for
your ſervant, or for a coach in a ſhower of
rain.—When by this means you have
found a ſeller of the ſum you want, you
will find yourſelf very often obliged to
give the turn of the market, that is, if it
is a doubt whether the market-price is ex-
actly that which he aſks, or rather inclined to fall $\frac{1}{8}$ beneath it, you muſt give
the turn of the ſcale to get your buſineſs
done; and this you will be obliged to do
nine times out of ten, if you employ a Broker — the better to underſtand the
price, obſerve the following table, which
is inſerted for the uſe of the many hundreds who read the public news papers,
without knowing the meaning of the odd
$\frac{1}{4}$'s annexed to the price of ſtocks:

is

$\frac{1}{8}$	is	2 s.	6 d.
$\frac{1}{4}$	———	5	0
$\frac{3}{8}$	———	7	6
$\frac{1}{2}$	———	10	0
$\frac{5}{8}$	———	12	6
$\frac{3}{4}$	———	15	0
$\frac{7}{8}$	———	17	6

By this table you find, that if you are afked 74 $\frac{5}{8}$ *per Cent.* for 3 *per Cent.* annuities, it means 74 *l.* 12 *s.* 6 *d.* which is the price you muſt give for 100 *l.* ſhare in them.

Having thus found the price, and agreed with the feller, you have only to give him your name, ſtyle or title, and place of abode ; it is his buſineſs (as the feller) to take care of the transfer, and prepare the receipt, only contrive to have the ſum you are to pay ready, and as near it as poſſible, in bank notes, ſo that you may not have more than four or five pounds to pay in caſh ; becauſe the hurry and buſtle is ſo great, that great inconveniences

veniences will arife in tranfacting your bufinefs if you do not obferve this rule.   If
you are well known on the Exchange,
and keep cafh at any Banker's in the
neighbourhood, your draught may do as
well as bank notes.   Another rule to be
obferved is, to keep in one part of the
room, till the transfer is prepared, that
you may be in readinefs to anfwer to your
name when called ; for if you are out of
the way, the clerks will not wait for you,
but proceed to other bufinefs : the tranf-
fer being prepared, and your name called,
you are to go to the clerk who has the
transfer book, who will fhew you the
form in which the feller has transfer'd the
fum   agreed for, to you, your   heirs,
affigns, &c. (which form I would advife
you to read the firft time, that you may be
thoroughly acquainted with the nature of
the affignment) you will then be directed
to fet your name to a form of acceptance
of the ftock transferred to you, the feller
having firft fet his hand to the transfer ;
                                    this

this done, the clerk witneſſes the printed
receipt, which the ſeller gives you, ſigned
by him ; and which you muſt keep as a
voucher for the transfer, 'till you have
received one dividend : the only reaſon
for this, that I could ever learn is, in
caſe the transfer ſhould by any means be
neglected to be poſted, and ſo the dividend warrant ſhould be made out in the
name of the old proprietor ; but this is a
caſe that happens ſo ſeldom (if ever) that
I think no perſon need be in great pain
about loſing a receipt of this kind*.
Having paid the ſum, and taken the
receipt,

---

* I muſt here give a caution againſt keeping theſe
receipts after you have received one dividend, for
they then become uſeleſs ; the caſhier having acknowledged your right in the fund by paying you a
dividend, and therefore they ſhould be deſtroyed ;
for by people's keeping them in families, (at their
death,) they ſometimes cauſe a great deal of confu-
ſion, eſpecially among the lower ſort of people ; and
prove

receipt, the whole bufinefs is tranfacted, and this is all, with refpect to a buyer.

Let us now explain the bufinefs of a feller, who, as has been remarked, has a little more to do, than the buyer.

As the largeft part of the national debt lies in the *3 per Cent. Annuities,* and as being the cheapeft, they are the moft dealt in, I fhall felect them as the propereft fund in which to give my explanation of the feller's bufinefs in transferring, or fel-ling out his property. Having found a

---

prove great difappointments to many, who think, in finding them, they have found a treafure. They immediately apply to the public offices from which the receipts have been iffued, and the clerks foon convince them, that they had better have been burnt: I hope, however, they pay nothing for examinations of this kind, fince every executor has an undoubted right, at proper hours, on producing the probate of the teftator's will, to examine the books, of any of the public funds (gratis) wherein he fufpects the teftator had any property.

pur-

purchafer (by the means before mentioned
in my directions to the buyer, the feller
muft get a piece of paper, about a quarter
of a fheet, and write on it his own name,
ftyle, and place of abode, with the fum
to be transfer'd, the fund it is to be
transfer'd out of, and the perfon's name
and defcription to whom it is to be
transfer'd ; to make this more clear, you
have here a form in the *3 per Cent*'s. which
will ferve for any other fund, ftriking
out only the words *3 per Cent. Annuities*,
and putting in its place, the particular
fund you have occafion to transfer*.

---

* If there is any little difference between one
public office and another, it is not material, and the
clerks are obliged to fet you right.

John

John Smith, Esq; of Knightsbridge,

500l. 3 per Cent. consolidated Bank Annuities.

To

James Goodman, Coal-Merchant, on Snow-Hill.

This

This paper you muſt deliver to the clerks that ſtand neareſt to, or under the letter, with which your name begins, and to which, you will be directed by the letters, which are painted at large on the wall; and by this regulation, and ſome laws in force, but neglected, it appears that the government deſigned that the proprietors ſhould manage their own buſineſs in the funds. Having delivered in your paper, the clerk examines your account; and if he finds you have the property you mention in your paper, he prepares the transfer, and as you are not a Broker, he, perhaps, will not call you when it is ready, and therefore your ſureſt way is to attend 'till it is done; and in the mean time to be making out the purchaſer's bill, which you are to do on a printed receipt, of theſe there are a ſufficient quantity always hanging up in all the offices; you have therefore only to aſk the clerks for them. The better to enable you to perform this part of the

buſineſs,

buſineſs, you have here a form of a receipt, filled up, which will ſerve you in
all caſes, only altering the ſums, and the
price, as occaſion requires : the parts
which are left blank in the receipt, and
are to be filled up by you, are thoſe printed in *Italics*.

Con-

$\pounds$ 74 12 6

Consolidated 3 *l. per Cent. Annuities, at* 74⅝.

Received this 21st Day of *May* 1761, of *James Godman* Coal Merchant on *Snow-Hill,* the Sum of *Seventy four Pounds Twelve Shillings and Sixpence,* being the Consideration for *One Hundred Pounds* Interest or Share in the Joint Stock of Three per Cent. Annuities, erected by an Act of Parliament of the Twenty-fifth Year of the Reign of King *George* II. (intitled, An Act for converting the several Annuities therein mentioned into several Joint Stocks of Annuities, transferrable at the Bank of England, to be charged on the Sinking Fund, together with the proportional Annuity at l. 3 per Cent. per Annum, attending the same, by me this Day tranferred to the said *James Godman.*

Witnefs my Hand,

John Smith.

Witnefs,
[Here the Clerk figns]

Having

Having figned your receipt, and the transfer being ready, you are to fign it in the book ; and then to deliver your receipt to the clerk, who (as foon as the purchafer has figned his acceptance in the book) will fign the receipt as a witnefs : this done deliver your receipt, and take your money of the purchafer, and the whole is finifhed.

There remains yet one difficulty, as eafy however to furmount, as the reft, which is, to caft up odd fums ; for it does not always happen that the fums to be bought, or fold, are even, as 100 *l.* or 500 *l.* but fometimes a mechanic, or a fervant, has faved up 20 or 30 pounds, and wants to buy in to the Annuities ; how fhall a common perfon reckon up 35 or 25 pounds of Anniuties at 74, without a Broker ? To make you eafy on this head, you have the following plain and infallible examples, which I am the more particular in, becaufe a

great

great many proprietors of large fums retail out thefe fmall fums, and buy them in again altogether in a capital fum; by which means they make great advantages, and with lefs rifk than in any other way.

RULES *for cafting up odd Quantities of* STOCK *at the current Price* per cent.

RULE I. If the quantity of STOCK you want to know the value of, is larger than the current price of one hundred, multiply that quantity by the price of one hundred, then divide by 100, the quotient will give you the value in pounds : then reduce the remainder (if any) by common reduction to fhillings—divide again by 100, and the quotient is the value in fhillings, and fo on to pence.—Obferve, that if from the feveral quotients you ftrike off the two laft figures to the right, as remainders to be reduced, it is the fame thing as dividing

by

by 100, and the figures to the left will
be pounds, if the quotient was ſo, and ſo
on to pence.

To prevent miſtakes, I ſhall give examples of both ways.

Example

Example of the firſt way.

What muſt I give for 126 *l.* in 3 *per Cent. Annuities,* at 74, that is to ſay, when 74 *l.* will buy 100 *l.*

	Example of the ſecond
126	way.
74	

$$
\begin{array}{r}
504 \\
882 \\
\hline
\end{array}
$$

£

100) 9324 (93

900

. 324

300

. 24

20

s.

100) 480 (4

400

. 80

12

d.

100) 960 (9

900

. 60

4

f.

100) 240 (2

200

. 40

Example of the ſecond way.

126

74

$$
\begin{array}{r}
504 \\
882 \\
\hline
\end{array}
$$

£ 93|24 ſtruck off.

20

s. 4|80

12

d. 9|60

4

f. 2|40

Anſwer £ 93 4 9 ½.

Anſwer £ 93 4 9 ½.

G

Rule

RULE II. When the quantity of STOCK
you want to know the value of, is fmaller
than the price *per Cent.* then multiply
that fmall quantity by the price *per Cent.*
and divide by 100, as before directed;
but if you are very careful to be exact,
the fhorteft and beft way is, to cut off
the two figures to the right; for which
reafon I fhall give the example of a fmall
fum, according to that method.

Example.

Example. What muſt I receive for 29 *l.* 3 *per Cent.*
Annuities, when the price is 74 *per Cent.*

74	If the price happens to be
29	an $\frac{1}{8}$, $\frac{3}{8}$, $\frac{5}{8}$, or $\frac{7}{8}$, in the
———	caſe where your quan-
666	tity is larger than the
148	price *per Cent.* take the
———	$\frac{1}{8}$, $\frac{3}{8}$, $\frac{5}{8}$, or $\frac{7}{8}$, part of the
£. 21|46	large ſum, and throw
20	it in after your multi-
———	plication, thus :
s. 9|20	
12	126
———	74 $\frac{5}{8}$ or 12 *s.* 6 *d.*
d. 2|40	———
4	504
———	882
f. 1|60	63 the $\frac{1}{2}$ or $\frac{4}{8}$ of 126
	15 : 15 $\frac{1}{8}$ making $\frac{5}{8}$
Anſwer 21 9 2$\frac{1}{4}$	£ 94|02 : 15
	20
	———
	·55
	12
	——— thus the fraction
	d. 6|60 is introduced.

Purſue this method even where the ſum
is ſmaller than the price *per Cent.* if it
conſiſts of two figures; but if it conſiſt
only of one figure, then the ſhorteſt way
is

is to multiply that, by the price *per Cent.*
and to take in the fraction in one line.

Example. What is the worth of 9 *l.* at 74 ⅝ *per
Cent?* By the Table already given, you know that ⅝
is 12 *s.* 6*d.* therefore work it thus:

```
        74  12   6
                 9
        ─────────────
  £ 6|71  12   6
        20
        ───
  s. 14|32
        12
        ───
  d. 3|90
         4
        ───
  f. 3|60
```
                        Anfwer £ 6 14   3¾

It is by this eafy and expeditious method, that fingle Blanks and Prizes are
caft up.

I muft here appeal to the candid and judicious, and beg leave to afk, If there is
                                       any

any thing in nature more eafy and fimple
than the tranfacting this bufinefs? the
whole of it does not take up above an
hour on the moft hurrying days of tranf-
ferring, and in the common run, not
above half the time; and if you have a
thoufand pounds to buy or fell, you gain,
or fave, which is the fame thing, 1 *l.* 5 *s.*
which is no inconfiderable premium for
half an hour's buftle in a crowd; befides
thofe who are difpofed to take advantage
of the variations in the funds, if they do
not act themfelves, can never make any
thing of a variation of $\frac{1}{4}$ *per Cent.* becaufe
the brokerage runs away with the profit.

The moft formidable obftacle to gentlemen's acting for themfelves at firft,
will be the impertinent behaviour of thofe
who are the fervants of the public, and
are well paid for their attendance; a man
of fpirit, however, will know how to
manage thefe gentlemen, and without
entering into any altercations with them,

G 3   will

will produce the authority of the laws,
as a check to all oppofition he may meet
with from them. With a view to affift
gentlemen in this point, and to fave them
the expence of purchafing the act of
parliament for raifing the fupplies for the
fervice of the current year, I have extracted the following claufe, which I leave to
the judicious to make the proper ufe of,
only obferving, that thofe who fhall give
occafion to any gentleman to make ufe of
it at all, give a fufpicion that (by their
places) being forbid to act as brokers,
they recommend their friends to particular brokers, and divide the profit with
them.

Claufe in an act of parliament lately
paffed, intitled, *An act for granting to his
Majefty an additional duty upon ftrong beer
and ale; and for raifing the fum of twelve
millions, by way of annuities, and a Lottery,* &c.

" And

" And be it further enacted, that no
" fee, reward or gratuity whatsoever,
" shall be demanded, or taken of any
" of his majesty's subjects, for receiving
" or paying the said contribution monies,
" or any of them ; or for any tallies or
" receipts concerning the same ; or for
" issuing the monies for paying the said
" several Annuities, or any of them ; or
" for any transfer of any sum, great or
" small, to be made in pursuance of this
" act, upon pain that any offender, or
" person offending, by taking or de-
" manding any such fee, reward, or gra-
" tuity, shall forfeit the-sum of twenty
" pounds to the party aggrieved, with
" full costs of suit, &c."———By a clause
in the same act, it is enacted, That the
transfer books shall be open at all season-
able times, wherein all persons may transfer, assign over, and accept stock ; and
in their absence, their attornies (lawfully
authorised) may do it for them ; but not
a word is said of Brokers.   In short the

legislature

legiflature has left the power and method
of transferring open to every body ; and
as free for a fervant, who has only ten
pounds to lay out, as for a merchant with
twenty thoufand ; and in feveral of the
money acts it is exprefsly enacted, that
the clerks in the transfer offices fhall
aid and affift ftrangers to transfer their
property.

If after all therefore, mankind will fhut
their eyes againft their own intereft, I can
only lament their blindnefs, and fit down
fatisfied with my own intention to do a
public good ; but not a little mortified
at its not producing the defired effect.
The ingenious Mrs. Centlivre, in her
comedy of the *Bold Stroke for a Wife*,
wrote many years ago, introduces a
Stock Broker, who, upon feeing two
gentlemen enter Jonathan's Coffee-houfe,
fays to his brethren, " I would fain bite
" that fpark in the brown coat, he comes
                                        " very

" very often into the Alley, but never
" employs a Broker." In this fhort fentence, fhe has happily expreffed the fen-
timents of the whole fraternity, and their
adherents; and has given us a hint, that
even in her days, fenfible people, faw
through the fallacy of employing Brokers, and tranfacted their own bufinefs;
and if this was the cafe then, how much
greater reafon is there for it at prefent,
when our funds are annually increafing,
and the brokerage confequently muft a-
mount to a prodigious fum ?

I fhall take my leave of this part of
my fubject with affuring my countrymen,
that if what I have advanced meets with
approbation, and encouragement, the
moft formidable oppofition fhall not abate
my zeal in their fervice; and if it be neceffary to give further inftructions, it fhall
not be wanting while a printing prefs is to
be found in this metropolis; in confe-

G 5   quence

quence of this declaration, all letters, and
inquiries relative to the funds, and all ob-
jections to my plan, if fent (poft paid) to
the publifher, fhall be duly taken notice
of in the fifth edition; and if it fhould
be found neceffary, as a further means of
putting the directions here given, in practice.——it is propofed to read a courfe
of lectures early in the enfuing winter, in
which the feveral branches of bufinefs in
the funds, will be explained by way of ex-
periment; for which purpofe, books, receipts, and all neceffaries as ufed at the
offices, will be prepared; and as foon as
a fufficient number of gentlemen are
thoroughly verfed in the manner of doing
their bufinefs, the author propofes to
attend them to the Bank, South-Sea,
and India Houfe, taking with him the
feveral acts of parliament, proper to en-
force a ready compliance in the clerks, to
do their proper duty, viz. to aid and affift
all perfons to transfer, and accept, ftocks,
                                                    and

and annuities.* Alſo ſome new and enter-
taining comic ſcenes in ſtock-jobbing
will be introduced, which could not be
inſerted here, without adding conſidera-
bly to the price of this little treatiſe.

Propoſals for theſe lectures will be delivered in a ſhort time ; and ſubſcriptions
taken in at the publiſher's——If the author finds a probability of meeting with
encouragement adequate to ſuch an en-
gagement.

I have already mentioned the conveniency of carrying Bank notes to buy
STOCK with, or if you are well known, of
drawing on your banker ; and here I muſt

---

* Several perſons have miſtaken the author's
meaning in this place ; and have ſent letters to him
requeſting his attendance to aſſiſt them in doing their
buſineſs at the public offices : to prevent any ſuch
application for the future, I muſt beg they will take
notice that the offer I make is to a collective body
of people ; and not to any one private perſon.

add

add a remark or two about taking Bank notes, and draughts.

When you are paid in Bank notes, for any STOCK you have fold, be careful to examine, if the notes are above a year old; for if they are, you fhould infift on having them examined, and marked in the office appointed for that purpofe in the Bank, before you take them: and if you are paid by the purchafer's draught on a banker, remember to go and receive it as foon as convenient, any time before five in the afternoon of the fame day; the reafon is obvious, viz. that a man may have cafh at his banker's in the morning, and may draw it all out before night; and therefore it is proper, according to the common courfe of bufinefs, to prefent the draught the fame day you receive it; otherwife, I am told, you have no remedy if payment fhould be refufed the next day.

But

But the fafeft way, when a purchafer propofes to give a draught on his banker by way of payment is, to defire him to draw, on the back of the receipt you are to give him as before directed ; for by this means you do not part with the receipt, till you have received your money at the banker's.

Of letters of attorney I fhall only obferve, that fuch as are proper, for all tranfactions in the funds, are to be had at the Bank, South-Sea and India-houfes ; and that people fhould be very careful what fort of letters of attorney they give, as fome are only for receiving of dividends, fome for buying, others for felling ; and general ones for buying and felling, and receiving of dividends, which convey a moft abfolute and unlimited power ; and have fometimes been given by ignorant people in the room of others, who have thereby put their properties into the hands of JOBBERS, who have loft

it

it all in the alley; amufing the proprietors in the mean time, by a punctual payment of the half yearly dividends.

As to the laws in force relating to Brokers, they lie within the jurifdiction of
the Right Honourable the Lord Mayor,
and court of Aldermen, who have enacted, that every perfon who acts as a Broker, within the city of London, fhall be
impowered fo to do, by being fworn in
before the Lord Mayor, and giving bond
for his fidelity, and good behaviour; and
likewife for the payment of 40 s. per
Annum, into the Comptroller's office.—
The form of this bond may be had at the
faid Comptroller's office in Guildhall, as
likewife a lift of the licenfed Exchange
Brokers, amongft which will be found a
few Stock-Brokers, but not one half of
the famous college, two thirds of which,
are not licenfed by any authority but their
own. On examining this bond, it will
appear

appear that Brokers are not to affemble in
'Change Alley, nor yet to have any property in the funds, they tranfact bufinefs
in (by commiffion). The reafons on which
thefe claufes are founded are very obvious, yet no Broker is reprimanded for
affembling in the Alley, nor yet for being poffeffed of, or contracting for ten
thoufand pounds, of any of the funds.—
One remark I cannot omit; which, if
the honorable court juft mentioned, (for
whom I have the moft profound refpect)
fhould view in the fame light, they will
probably alter the manner of admitting
Brokers.——The Broker, on his admif-
fion, gives only his own perfonal bond,
in the penal fum of 500 l for his fidelity to the public; but he finds the fecurity of a fubftantial houfekeeper, for
the 40 s. per Annum payable to the
city: How unequal this meafure!——
A Broker, during his whole life, cannot owe the city above 150 l.—but

he

he may in an hour forfeit the 500 l. to the public *.

Having thus given the plaineſt, and moſt ample directions for tranſacting the buſineſs in the funds, not founded on ſpeculation, but on the experience of a year's practice, I ſhall cloſe this chapter with the following tables.

---

* Some Exchange Brokers are entruſted for months together with merchandiſe to a very great amount.

A TABLE

A TABLE, fhewing the Days and Hours of Transferring the following STOCKS and ANNUITIES, and the Time of paying the Dividends.

Amount of each Capital.

	£	s.	d.	Transfer Days.
BANK STOCK - - - -	10.780.000	—	—	
Ann. 3 per Cent. red.	17.701.323	16	4	
Ditto Confolidated - -	21.627.821	5	1¼	Tu.Wed.Thur.Frid.
Ditto 1726 - - - - -	1.000.000	—	—	
Three 1-half 1756 - -	1.500.000	—	—	Tuefd. and Thurfd.
Ditto 1758 - - - - -	4.500.000	—	—	Mond.Wednef. Frid.
Four per Cent. 1760 -	8.240.000	—	—	Tu.Wed.Thur.Frid.

Dividends due on Bank Stock and Three per Cent. reduced on the 5th of April, and 10th of October, on the reft the 5th of January, and 5th of July.

Amount of each Capital.

	£	s.	d.	Transfer Days.
SOUTH SEA STOCK -	3.662.784	8	6	Mond.Wednef. Frid.
Old Annuities - - -	12.404.270	—	—	
New Annuities - - -	8.958.255	2	10	Tuefd.Thurf.Saturd.
Three per Cent. 1751	2.100.000	—	—	

South Sea Stock, New Annuities, and Three per Cent. Dividends due on the 5th of January, and the 5th of July, Old Annuities the 5th of April, and 10th of October.

Amount of each Capital.

	£	s.	d.	Transfer Days.
INDIA STOCK - - -	3.200.000	—	—	Tuef. Thurf. Saturd.
Annuities - - - - -	3.000.000	—	—	Mond. Wednef. Frid.

Dividends due on India Stock, 5th of January and 5th of July. Ditto — Annuities, 5th of April — 10th of Oct.

HOURS of TRANSFERRING STOCK at the

BANK from - 9 to 12
SOUTH Sea Houfe 9 to 1 } Dividends paid from { 9 to 11 and 1 to 3
INDIA Houfe - 9 to 1 } { 9 to 12
HOLIDAYS excepted. { 9 to 12 and 3 to 5

☞ At the INDIA Houfe no Transfers are made after Twelve o'Clock on Saturdays, and no Dividends in the Afternoon.

N. B. The transfer books are generally fhut for a month before the time of paying dividends.

HOLIDAYS

HOLIDAYS are kept at the Exchequer, Stamp-Office, Excise-Office, Custom-House, Bank, East-India, and South-Sea House, on the following Days, viz.

Days.		Holidays.	Days.		Holidays.
January	1	Circumcifion	July	15	St. Swithin
	6	Epiphany		25	St. James
	25	‡ St. Paul			
	30	K. Ch. I. Martyr.			
February	2	Purif. V. Mary	August	1	Lammas Day
	3	Shrove Tuefday		24	St. Bartholomew
	4	Afh Wednefday			
	14	Valentine			
	24	St. Matthias			
March	1	St. David	September	2	‡London burnt
	20	Good Friday		14	Holy Rood
	23	Eafter Monday		21	St. Matthew
	24	Eafter Tuefday		29	St. Michael
	25	Lady Day			
April	23	St. George	October	18	St. Luke
	25	St. Mark		26	K. Geo.III. procl.
	26	D. Cumberl. born		28	St. Sim. & St. Jude
	30	Afcenfion Day.			
May	1	St. Philip & Jac.	November	1	All Saints
	11	Whit. Monday		2	All Souls
	12	Whit. Tuefday		4	K. William born
	13	Whit. Wednefday		5	Powder Plot
	29	‡ K. Ch. II. Reft.		9	‡Ld.Mayor'sDay.
				28	Qu. Eliz. Accef.
				30	Prfs.Wales born
June	4	‡KingGeo.III. born	December	21	St. Thomas
	10	Prfs. Amelia born		25	Chriftmas Day
	11	St. Barnabas		26	St. Stephen
	24	St. John Bapt.		27	St. John
	29	St. Peter & Paul		28	Innocents

If the Holidays marked thus ‡ fall on a Sunday, they are kept the next Day.

N. B. At the Custom-House there is no Holiday on Valentine, St. David, Shrove Tuefday, Eafter-Wednefday, Duke of Cumberland's Birth Day, Whit-Wednefday, St. Swithin, Lammas-Day, Fire of London, or Holy Rood.

At the South-Sea, Bank and East-India Houfes, there is no Holiday on Valentine, S. David, S. Swithin, or Holy Rood.

CHAP. IV.

Giving an account of the method of raifing the annual Supplies granted by Parliament, for defraying the public expences of the State.—— Of the manner of fubfcribing, and of buying and felling Subfcription Receipts, for 3 per Cent. Annuities, and Lottery Tickets. Diftinction betwixt Subfcription paid in upon in full, or only paid in up to the time of fale ; called (in the language of 'Change-Alley) LIGHT-HORSE and HEAVY-HORSE.—— Difference betwixt SUBSCRIPTION and OMNIUM, vulgarly known by the names of SCRIP. and OMNIUM GATHERUM.

THE method of raifing the fupplies granted by Parliament, for carrying on the war, &c. for fome years paft, has been by Annuities transferrable at the Bank of England ; fometimes with, and at other times without, a Lottery.

When

When the parliament have voted thefe
fupplies, and refolved on ways and means
of raifing them, a fubfcription is fet on
foot, and is either open to the public, in
which cafe every refponfable perfon is at
liberty to apply, by a proper letter to the
firft commiffioner of the treafury, for
leave to be admitted to be a contributor,
naming in his letter, the fum he defires
to contribute ; or elfe it is private, that
is to fay, a certain number of perfons of
fortune, have agreed to be anfwerable
for the whole fum to be fubfcribed : and
have made the required depofit. In this
cafe the only ftep to be taken, by thofe
who are not of the number juft mentioned, is, to apply to them for fuch part of
the fubfcription as you want, which, if
you are a particular friend, they will,
perhaps, fpare you without any premium,
or for a very fmall one; for it is not to be
prefumed, that any fmall number of men
who have fubfcribed for the whole fum
to be raifed, intend, or can keep it, but
that

that they purpofe to include in their fubfcription, all their friends and acquaint-
ance.   Sometimes the fubfcription lies
open to the Public at the Bank, or at the
Exchequer, and then every perfon is allowed to fubfcribe what he thinks proper ;
and if, upon cafting up the whole, there
is a furplus fubfcribed, as has generally
been the cafe, the fum each fubfcriber
has fubfcribed, is reduced in a juft proportion, fo as to make in the whole the
fum granted by Parliament.

As foon as conveniently may be, after
the fubfcription is clofed, receipts are made
out and delivered to the fubfcribers, for
the feveral fums by them fubfcribed : and
for the conveniency of fale, every fubfcriber of a confiderable fum has fundry
receipts, for different proportions of his
whole fum, by which means he can the
readier part with what fum he thinks proper ; and a form of affignment is drawn
upon the back of the receipt, which being

ing figned and witneffed, transfers the
property to a purchafer.

The firft depofit is generally of 15
per Cent. and is made on or about the
time of fubfcribing ; the fecond at about
a month after, and fo on till the whole is
paid in, which is generally in October ;
each monthly payment being either 10 or
15 *per Cent.* Thofe who chufe to pay in
the whole fum before the appointed days
of payment, are allowed 3 *per Cent.* from
the time of fuch payment to October.
The fubfcription receipts thus paid in full,
are called in the Alley, HEAVY-HORSE,
becaufe the gentlemen of the Alley can
make greater advantage than 3 *per Cent.*
by the LIGHT-HORSE, and therefore
will not give near fo good a price for the
heavy ; naye, fome of them will abfolutely
have nothing to do with it, for this reafon ; that they can buy a thoufand pounds,
LIGHT-HORSE, (with one payment
made) for the fame money as one hundred

dred pounds heavy, and by buying the light, they have an opportunity of sporting with, and gaining a profit on, a nominal thousand, for the same money, that it would cost to buy an hundred, heavy.

LIGHT HORSE therefore, is the commodity to JOBB with, and opens a most extensive scene of it; to illustrate this, I shall go no further than the scheme by which the supplies are raised for the current year.

It consists of *3 per Cent. Annuities*, transferrable at the Bank, an annuity certain, of 1 l. 2 s. 6 d. *per Cent.* for 99 years; and a lottery ticket at ten pounds; the two last articles are designed as (*douceurs*) or rewards, for subscribing to the *3 per Cent's.* The premium, or profit upon the whole, to the subscribers, will be more or less, according to the value of the several articles, which vary almost every day; few of the subscribers, however,

ever, keep their whole fubfcription un-
divided; and therefore as each article is
faleable apart, there is always a fufficient
quantity of each in the market, as foon
as the receipts are out, (which is generally after the fecond payment) and happens
moft commonly in February: the receipts
for the *3 per Cent. Annuities*, are called
by the Brokers, SCRIP. and LIGHT-
HORSE; that is, they are convenient
troops; and do not coft much to main-
tain; and may be difbanded with much
greater eafe than the HEAVY HORSE.

The conveniency of LIGHT-HORSE,
or SCRIP. is this; that, in the month of
March, for inftance, juft after the fecond
payment, a perfon may buy a receipt for
500 *l*. SCRIP. for 25 *l*. the method of
reckoning which is thus; fuppofe the
current price is 75 *per Cent*; (which actually was the price in February laft)
this is 25 *per Cent*. below par; and as
the purchafer buys the SCRIP. by itfelf,
without

without the *douceurs* that accompanied
it, he muſt be allowed the diſcount, *viz.*
25 *per Cent.* out of the payments already
made, becauſe he is to continue paying
in at par, in the ſame manner as if he
had received the *douceurs*; therefore the
method of making out a bill for 500 *l.*
Scrip. with two payments made upon it,
will be as follows :

A, ſells to B. 500 *l.* Scrip.
at 75 *per Cent.* on which
he has made two payments
of 15 *per Cent.* each — } £ 150

B, not having the Lottery
Tickets, nor the Long
Annuities, which are the
Douceurs, muſt be al-
lowed 25 *per Cent.* the } £ 125 to be deducted.
difference bewixt the cur-
rent price of 3 *per Cents.*
and par. ——

Ballance to be paid to A.
for the receipt — } £ 25

H   From

From this ftate of the cafe it appears, that
B. becomes poffeffed of 500 *l.* Scrip.
for 25 *l.* which he may therefore juftly
call Light Horse ; and the great profit
of Scrip. bought on thefe eafy terms is,
that, if a little rife happens, you make
the fame advantage of 1, 2, or *3 per
Cent.* on the nominal fum, as if you
had actually paid in the whole ; and can
likewife find more purchafers for your
receipts ; for no man who buys with a
view of felling again, when a favourable
opportunity happens, will chufe to give
375 *l.* (which is the value when all is paid
in for that, which he can buy for 25 *l.*

It is eafy to conceive what a vaft field is
opened by this means for Jobbing, as a
man poffeffed of 500 *l.* in cafh, may
purchafe 10,000 *l.* after the fecond payment ; and if he cannot fell it again to
advantage before the next payment comes
on, he may put it out to nurfe, that is,
depofit it in the hands of fome monied
man,

man, who, for a proper confideration, will pay in upon it, and keep it as his fecurity, 'till the proprietor has an opportunity of felling it to advantage; which he will do fooner or later, if he has any fkill in,—private letters from the Hague*, &c. This part of JOBBING is, however, the leaft to be found fault with of any, becaufe every man has an undoubted right to buy and fell as often as he thinks proper; but then it may reafonably be fuppofed, that the great advantages arifing to the Brokers from this conftant circulation of SCRIP. joined to the opportunity every man has, of fporting in the Alley with fmall fums, have co-operated to obftruct the carrying into execution many better fchemes for raifing the fupplies;

---

* When a man carries his fhirt to a fhop to borrow money on it, we ufually fay, he has pawned it, and call the lender, a Pawnbroker; but when a gentleman carries his SCRIP. to nurfe, 'tis only faid, he has depofited it at his Banker's.

becaufe

becaufe, from the nature of them, they would have been open to the public, and could not have paffed through the hands of the Brokers, nor their adherents. The year 1756, or 1757, I think, furnifhed us with an inftance of this kind, when a fcheme for raifing the fupplies on a new plan, admirably calculated to prevent the increafe of the national debt, and as advantageous to the public, as any that has fince been accepted, lay at the Bank for feveral days unfilled; and was obliged to be laid afide, for no other reafon that ever I could find, but, becaufe the Brokers univerfally cried it down, and advifed all their clients to have nothing to do with it, for this obvious reafon; that the whole tranfaction was to be betwixt the people, and the government; and thefe gentlemen could reap little or no profit from it.

Lottery Tickets, are likewife divided into LIGHT and HEAVY HORSE; the
former

former of which anſwering the ſame pur-
poſes as SCRIP. it is needleſs to ſay any
thing further on this head.

The long Annuities, which make part
of the preſent ſcheme, vary in their prices,
like the reſt; they were in February laſt
at 22 years purchaſe; but now they are
26; all the funds having roſe conſider-
ably, (on the rumor of an approaching
peace) ſince the greateſt part of this work
went to the preſs; ſo that the author
hopes an allowance will be made for his
making his calculations of 3 *per Cent's.*
&c. much below the preſent riſe, which
he could not foreſee. By the neareſt
computation I can make, I am humbly
of opinion, that the intrinſic value of an
annuity of $\frac{1}{8}$ or 1 l. 2 s. 6 d. for 99 years
is, 24 years purchaſe, at the preſent rate
of intereſt.

OMNIUM is the whole ſubſcription un-
divided; and is known in the Alley by

the

the name of Omnium Gatherum, a
cant phrafe for, all together ; this was at
par in February laft ; and was thus made
out.

	l.	s.	d.
Scrip.　　　——————	75	0	0
Premium on Tickets at 10l. 13 s.	0	13	0
Long Annuities at 22 years purchafe	24	15	0
	100	8	0

The 8 s. difference, is an allowance to be
made for the conveniency of buying the
articles feparate, each article being worth
a little more by itfelf, than when joined
to the reft, under the title of Omnium
Gatherum.

C H A P.

CHAP. V.

Of India Bonds.—Form of making out bills for
selling of them; with new Tables of Interest
calculated at 5 per Cent. which is the interest
they now bear.—Some account of Navy Bills,
and Life Annuities; and directions how to
avoid the losses that frequently happen from
the destruction of Bank-Notes, India-Bonds,
and other public securities for money,—by
fire, and other accidents

INDIA bonds are the most
convenient and profitable secu-
rity any person can be possessed
of, who has any quantity of cash un-
employed, but which he knows not how
soon he may have occasion for; the
utility and advantage of these bonds is
so well known to the Merchants, and
Traders of the city of London, that it is
wholly unnecessary to enlarge upon it;

the

the intereft they carry at prefent has brought them to a confiderable premium, by which it appears that money is not worth quite *5 per Cent.* at prefent, though I believe fix months fince, it was fully worth it. There is as little trouble with an India Bond, as with a Bank Note: it is not indeed current in the common courfe of bufinefs, but may always be fold in office-hours, at any of the public offices, as well as at Jonathan's Coffee-houfe; and the method of making out the bill is this.—Take a quarter of a fheet of paper, and write,

Sold Sir Friendly Wilfon, Apr. 20, 1761.

One India Bond (B. 207)	100	0	0
Intereft 2 months 17 days	1	1	$3\frac{3}{4}$
Premium	2	0	0
£ 103	1	$3\frac{3}{4}$

Under this write a common receipt.

When

When you want to buy, you have no further trouble than to agree on the price, for the feller is to make out the bill.

Thefe bonds are ufually for 100 l. each; and the feller receives the intereft of the purchafer, up to the day he fells.

Upon looking over moft of the printed intereft books, I have found them needlefsly prolix, on the fubject of India Bonds; for when you have got a table of the intereft from one day, to thirty, and from 1 month, to 12, you can with as much eafe add together the months and odd days you want, (when under one point of view) as turn over eight or ten pages to find 84, or 90, or any other number of days. But if the Brokers fhould object to this, that they have not time to caft up two fums inftead of one, I can only anfwer, that I write not for them, (unlefs it be for their amendment) and that I afk not theirs, but the public's patronage, for whofe fervice the fol-

H 5 lowing

lowing five tables are inferted. I have
placed the days in fucceffive order, and
the months following them in each table ;
and have carried the calculations as far as
500 l. or five Bonds, (by doubling of
which, the intereft of any intermediate
number of Bonds may be found from
two to 10,) which is as high as moft intereft books have carried them ; and in
order to attain this, the author of one of
them labours through 76 pages.

T A B L E S

TABLES of INTEREST on INDIA-BONDS, at 5 *per Cent*.

100 *l.* for

	l.	*s.*	*d.*			*l.*	*s.*	*d.*
1 Day	—		$3\frac{1}{4}$	22 Days	—	6	—	$\frac{1}{4}$
2 Days	—		$6\frac{1}{2}$	23 Days	—	6	$3\frac{1}{2}$
3 Days	—		$9\frac{3}{4}$	24 Days	—	6	$6\frac{3}{4}$
4 Days	—	1	1	25 Days	—	6	10
5 Days	—	1	$4\frac{1}{4}$	26 Days	—	7	$1\frac{1}{4}$
6 Days	—	1	$7\frac{1}{2}$	27 Days	—	7	$4\frac{3}{4}$
7 Days	—	1	11	28 Days	—	7	8
8 Days	—	2	2	29 Days	—	7	$11\frac{1}{2}$
9 Days	—	2	$5\frac{1}{4}$	30 Days	—	8	$2\frac{1}{2}$
10 Days	—	2	$8\frac{1}{2}$	a Month	—	8	4
11 Days	—	3	—	2 Months		16	8
12 Days	—	3	$3\frac{1}{4}$	3 Months	1	5	—
13 Days	—	3	$6\frac{1}{2}$	4 Months	1	13	4
14 Days	—	3	10	5 Months	2	1	8
15 Days	—	4	$1\frac{1}{4}$	6 Months	2	10	—
16 Days	—	4	$4\frac{1}{2}$	7 Months	2	18	4
17 Days	—	4	$7\frac{3}{4}$	8 Months	3	6	8
18 Days	—	4	11	9 Months	3	15	—
19 Days	—	5	$2\frac{1}{4}$	10 Months	4	3	4
20 Days	—	5	$5\frac{3}{4}$	11 Months	4	11	8
21 Days	—	5	9	1 Year	5	—	—

T A-

TABLES of INTEREST on INDIA-BONDS, at 5 *per Cent.*

200 *l.* for

	l.	*s.*	*d.*			*l.*	*s.*	*d.*
1 Day	—	—	6 ½		22 Days	—	12	—
2 Days	—	1	1		23 Days	—	12	7
3 Days	—	1	7 ½		24 Days	—	13	1
4 Days	—	2	2		25 Days	—	13	8
5 Days	—	2	8 ½		26 Days	—	14	2
6 Days	—	3	3		27 Days	—	14	9
7 Days	—	3	10		28 Days	—	15	5
8 Days	—	4	4		29 Days	—	15	11
9 Days	—	4	11		30 Days	—	16	6
10 Days	—	5	5		a Month	—	16	8
11 Days	—	6	—		2 Months	1	13	4
12 Days	—	6	6		3 Months	2	10	—
13 Days	—	7	1		4 Months	3	6	8
14 Days	—	7	8		5 Months	4	3	4
15 Days	—	8	2		6 Months	5	—	—
16 Days	—	8	9		7 Months	5	16	8
17 Days	—	9	3		8 Months	6	13	4
18 Days	—	9	10		9 Months	7	10	—
19 Days	—	10	4 ½		10 Months	8	6	8
20 Days	—	10	11 ½		11 Months	9	3	4
21 Days	—	11	6		a Year	10	—	—

T A-

TABLES of INTEREST on INDIA-BONDS,
at 5 *per Cent.*

300 *l.* for

	l.	*s.*	*d.*			*l.*	*s.*	*d.*
1 Day	—	—	9¾	22 Days	—	18	—⁷⁄₄
2 Days	—	1	7½	23 Days	—	18	10½
3 Days	—	2	5½	24 Days	—	19	8¼
4 Days	—	3	3	25 Days	1	—	6
5 Days		4	1	26 Days	1	1	4¼
6 Days	—	4	11	27 Days	1	2	2¼
7 Days	—	5	9	28 Days	1	3	—
8 Days	—	6	6½	29 Days	1	3	10
9 Days	—	7	4¼	30 Days	1	4	7¾
10 Days	—	8	2	a Month	1	5	—
11 Days	—	9	—	2 Months	2	10	—
12 Days	—	9	10	3 Months	3	15	—
13 Days	—	10	8	4 Months	5	—	—
14 Days	—	11	6	5 Months	6	5	—
15 Days	—	12	3¾	6 Months	7	10	—
16 Days	—	13	1½	7 Months	8	15	—
17 Days	—	13	11	8 Months	10	—	—
18 Days	—	14	9	9 Months	11	5	—
19 Days	—	15	7¾	10 Months	12	10	—
20 Days	—	16	5½	11 Months	13	15	—
21 Days	—	17	3¼	a Year	15	—	—

T A-

TABLES of INTEREST on INDIA-BONDS, at 5 *per Cent.*

400 *l.* for

	l.	*s.*	*d.*		*l.*	*s.*	*d.*
1 Day —		1	1	22 Days	1	4	1
2 Days —		2	2	23 Days	1	5	2
3 Days —		3	3	24 Days	1	6	3
4 Days —		4	4	25 Days	1	7	4
5 Days —		5	5	26 Days	1	8	5
6 Days —		6	6	27 Days	1	9	7
7 Days —		7	8	28 Days	1	10	8
8 Days —		8	9	29 Days	1	11	9
9 Days —		9	10	30 Days	1	12	10
10 Days —		10	11	a Month	1	13	4
11 Days —		12	—	2 Months	3	6	8
12 Days —		13	1	3 Months	5	—	—
13 Days —		14	2	4 Months	6	13	4
14 Days —		15	4	5 Months	8	6	8
15 Days —		16	5	6 Months	10	—	—
16 Days —		17	6	7 Months	11	13	4
17 Days —		18	7	8 Months	13	6	8
18 Days —		19	8	9 Months	15	—	—
19 Days	1	—	9	10 Months	16	13	4
20 Days	1	1	11	11 Months	18	6	8
21 Days	1	3	—	a Year	20	—	—

T A-

TABLES of INTEREST on INDIA-BONDS, at 5 per Cent.

500 l. for

	l.	s.	d.		l.	s.	d.
1 Day —		1	4 $\frac{1}{4}$	22 Days	1	10	1 $\frac{1}{2}$
2 Days —		2	8 $\frac{1}{2}$	23 Days	1	11	6
3 Days —		4	1 $\frac{3}{4}$	24 Days	1	12	10 $\frac{1}{2}$
4 Days —		5	5 $\frac{1}{2}$	25 Days	1	14	2 $\frac{3}{4}$
5 Days —		6	10	26 Days	1	15	7 $\frac{1}{4}$
6 Days —		8	2 $\frac{1}{2}$	27 Days	1	16	11 $\frac{3}{4}$
7 Days —		9	7	28 Days	1	18	4 $\frac{1}{4}$
8 Days —		10	11 $\frac{1}{2}$	29 Days	1	19	8 $\frac{1}{2}$
9 Days —		12	3 $\frac{1}{4}$	30 Days	2	1	1
10 Days —		13	8 $\frac{1}{4}$	a Month	2	1	8
11 Days —		15	— $\frac{3}{4}$	2 Months	4	3	4
12 Days —		16	5 $\frac{1}{4}$	3 Months	6	5	—
13 Days —		17	9 $\frac{1}{2}$	4 Months	8	6	8
14 Days —		19	2	5 Months	10	8	4
15 Days	1	—	6 $\frac{1}{2}$	6 Months	12	10	—
16 Days	1	1	11	7 Months	14	11	8
17 Days	1	3	3 $\frac{1}{4}$	8 Months	16	13	4
18 Days	1	4	7 $\frac{3}{4}$	9 Months	18	15	
19 Days	1	6	— $\frac{1}{2}$	10 Months	20	16	8
20 Days	1	7	4 $\frac{1}{4}$	11 Months	22	18	4
21 Days	1	8	9	a Year	25	—	—

Of

Of Navy Bills I have only to obferve, that they are delivered from the Navy, and Victualling Offices, to fuch perfons as contract with them for fundry provifions and ftores for the fervice of our fleets; and as thefe people are very often in want of their money, before thefe bills are paid off by the government, they bring them into the Alley to be difcounted; and to this end they are made out with blank affignments, fo as to be fold without any difficulty. The price of difcounting them varies with the other public fecurities; but has lately been about 9 *per Cent.* They have been paid off for fome time paft, within twelve months after date, but this is not always infallibly to be expected; they carry four *per Cent.* intereft, fix months after date, but none till then. They are dangerous things to lofe, on account of the blank affignment; and not being a general commodity, becaufe they are moftly for large fums, they are confined to a few hands at J——'s; and to the publc

in

in general, for whofe fervice I write; they are upon the whole not the moft elligible commodity; though to fome particular people, who can afford to lie out of their money fome time, and have large fums to fpare for this purpofe, they are very advantageous.

Life Annuities depend fo much on the age and conftitution of the purchafer, in which moft fellers are extremely nice and difficult, that it is impoffible to give any unexceptionable rules about them; for if you want to buy, and carry the niceft calculations with you, that ever appeared in print, you will not find one feller that will regard them; on the contrary, he will rather chufe to go by his own opinion of your life, from a review of your perfon; and a ftrict enquiry into the general manner of your living; after which, if he likes you, (which he will feldom do, unlefs he has reafon to think you have paffed through

the

the hands of some of the celebrated Quacks) he will demand five or six years purchase more than you ought to give, according to the most esteemed calculations, especially if he gives you government-security. Upon the whole, Life Annuities are very dear purchases, and ought to be discouraged by every well-wisher to posterity; since they serve only to increase the incomes, and nourish in luxury, the decayed carcasses of Old Maids and Batchelors, at the expence of their fortunes, which at their deaths generally pass into the hands of the Israelites, instead of being bequeathed (as they ought) to strengthen the hands of industry, to comfort and support the widow and orphan, and to relieve poor and needy relations.

I shall here subjoin a few directions to avoid the frequent losses that are sustained by the destruction of Bank Notes, India Bonds, &c. which however simple they may be, will be found not the less useful,

ful, and may not have entered in the heads of thofe who ftand moft in need of them.

A great many people have iron chefts, and a fort of iron caves placed in brickwork, in their cellars; thefe, no doubt, are very fecure; but there are numbers who are not fituated in places where thefe conveniences are to be had; and if they are, perhaps cannot afford them, yet they have often, in the courfe of bufinefs, Bank Notes, India Bonds, and other fecurities, the lofs of which, may be more fatal to them, than to the rich who have thefe means of fecurity: thefe therefore I advife to take the numbers, and principal contents, of all public fecurities for money, in a fmall memorandum, or pocket-book, to be kept always about them, fo that if they efcape with only their cloaths from a fire, they may be able to fwear to, and recover their property. What makes me the

more

more particular in giving this direction is, that I have obferved that feveral tradef-men when they go out of town, lock up their notes, and the books in which they are entered, in the fame compting-houfe, and fometimes in the fame defk, than which nothing can be more abfurd : nay, even when at home, it is much better to have fuch a memorandum about you, as you have thereby the lefs to think of, and the lefs hazard to run, in cafe of fire. I think this hint might in many cafes be extended even to an abftract of debts; but this I fubmit to better judge-ments, as not knowing whether fuch an abftract, would be valid in a court of equity. I have only to add, that I wifh my labours may prove beneficial to all proprietors of the funds, and thofe who may hereafter become fo, that I may have the fatisfaction of having done a public good to this my native country.

I

I cannot conclude thefe fheets better, than by returning my fincereft thanks to the right noble, and honorable per- fonages, who were fo obliging (on my expreffing my fears about publifhing a work of this kind) as to promife me their intereft, and fupport, againft any oppofition, infult, or outrage, that I might meet with from the alley, fince, to this encouragement, and the public fa- vor, I ftand indebted for the fuccefs of three editions of this little piece.

A P-

APPENDIX.

SOME letters having been ſent to the Publiſher's, deſiring me to give an account of the nature of Banking; and alſo of the Sinking Fund. —In compliance with the requeſts of the writers, I ſhall here give a ſhort account of both, ſo as to ſatisfy the curious, and render them intelligible to every one; but a full and particular account of them would require a ſeparate treatiſe; and I am afraid upon the whole, would ſit but heavily upon the reader's hands.

The art or trade of banking was brought over to England by foreigners; and ſome authors ſay, by Italians.—The common buſineſs of theſe bankers was, the exchange of bills for money; whether

ther thefe bills were inland, or foreign,
which exchange, in cafe the bills were
inland, was then, and is ftill termed,
Difcounting of bills. But when the bills
are foreign, they are called bills of Exchange; becaufe they are current in
trade, and as good as cafh, allowing only the common courfe of exchange betwixt the value of fpecie in the different
countries, where the drawer, and the
perfon drawn upon refide; and bankers
being fuppofed to have a general corref-
pondence in the commercial world, bills
of exchange paffing from one nation to
another, moft properly fell under their
cognizance, as being the moft convenient to them, who might frequently have
occafion to remit money to feveral parts,
in the place of which, they could more
profitably fubftitute thefe bills of exchange; thus it became moft advantageous for bankers to buy them; and
this branch of trade ftill forms a very
confiderable

confiderable part of the bufinefs of fome
bankers.

Another article they formerly dealt in
was the buying and felling of bullion,
and of wrought gold and filver, which
I fuppofe gave rife to the uniting in one
fhop, the trade of a goldfmith and
banker—for we find moft of the eminent
bankers of the laft century were gold-
fmiths.—By the ftatute of 6th of William and Mary, the bank (which is no
more than a corporation of bankers)
amongft other privileges allowed them,
are to deal in gold and filver, and may
fell goods pledged to them, if not redeemed in three months. By length of
time, and the increafe of the national
debt, the bank and private bankers have
changed, or totally thrown afide many
branches of their bufinefs; and the principal concerns of the bank at prefent are,
the iffuing of notes, in exchange for fpecie;
the keeping of gentlemen, and mer-
mer-

chants cash, which they are always ready to deliver on demand; and the aiding and affifting the government in receiving contributions for public fubfcriptions; the keeping of transfer books open, as already mentioned; and the paying and diftributing the intereft of the feveral governments fecurities. The firft of thefe articles muft greatly enrich the bank as a corporation; for thefe notes are now defervedly in the fame repute as cafh, even in many foreign parts *, as well as at home; and people often keep thefe notes by them for a long fpace of time, fometimes for years without exchanging them; and even

---

* It is very remarkable, but at the fame time no lefs true, that Bank Notes are eagerly fought after, and rather bear a premium at Bruffels, which may be almoft called an enemy's country; whereas amongft our good friends the Dutch, they are under par, particularly at Middleburgh, a famous city in Zealand.

I   then

then probably they may exchange them with private perfons.—Let us then fuppofe, that only 50,000 *l*. worth of notes do not return into the bank for fpecie in lefs than fix months, after they are iffued, the bank in this interim may make a very confiderable advantage of the cafh originally paid in for thefe notes.

It is not, however, my defign to make any calculation of their profits, which they merit, were it ever fo great, for I think I may venture to fay, (without being charged with partiality as an Englifhman) that the Bank of England is the beft bank in Europe.—My reafon for explaining the profits arifing from the iffuing of notes for cafh, is to fhew that thefe profits have induced private people to endeavour to put their notes upon the fame footing*, fo that one part of the bufinefs

---

* It is become a common practice lately, and calls aloud for redrefs, that inconfiderable tradefmen refiding

buſineſs of private bankers is, to deliver
out their notes for caſh, and from this
ariſes part of their ſubſiſtence; for while
theſe notes remain in particular hands,
or can be circulated ſo as not to return
home for whole months together, the
bankers enjoy the ſame privilege and
profit as the bank, in proportion to the
notes they iſſue.——The ſame profits ariſe
from keeping people's caſh. I have been
aſked how a banker could find his account in permitting a broker to put
his money into their hands perhaps on
Saturday afternoon, and to draw it out
the Monday morning following, ſince

ſiding in London, travel into the ſeveral counties
of England to take orders, and there take up caſh
upon their notes, which are handſomely engraved
on copper-plates, which ignorant country ſhop-
keepers imagine are as good as the Bank, under this
form; but ſometimes to their coſt they find that
payment is ſtopt; and that it would have been
much ſafer to have ſent up the money to their cor-
reſpondents by the ſtage-waggon, or any ſuch convenience.

there is a certain expence, and lofs of time, without any apparent profit ? In anfwer to which, let it be obferved, that bankers do not in general confider the profit they gain on the account of any individual, but the gain upon the whole.—So that fuppofing a banker receives in any one day 60,000 *l.* and is drawn upon only for 30,000 *l.* the ballance of cafh remaining in his hands at five in the afternoon (the time they fhut up) is 30,000 *l.* and a broker's 1000 *l.* contributes to the forming this ballance, which a fkilful banker will know how to employ to advantage, if he has it only one day in his hands ; but if upon an average a banker has 200,000 *l.* in his hands more than is called for, for weeks together, it is eafy to conceive, that fuch a man will foon get rich.—Another, and perhaps as confiderable a branch of bufinefs as any, amongft the bankers near the alley is, the taking in various kinds of papers in pawn—Such as Scrip. Omnium,

nium, Long Annuities, &c.—But this part of their traffic, it will take up too much room fully to unravel in this Appendix;—I shall therefore make only one remark, which is, that it is impossible to distinguish which are the most useful to each other; the brokers to some of the bankers near the alley, or these bankers to the brokers.

The nature of the Sinking Fund I shall endeavour to give as brief, and as clear an idea of as possible.

All sums of money that have at any time been raised by authority of parliament for the public service, are to be considered as national debts, various interests for which debts are annually paying to the public; and will continue to be so paid, 'till the said debts are redeemed, or paid off, by the same authority by which they were contracted; and to secure the payment of the said

I 3   interest,

interest, the monies arising from several
duties, and customs payable into the King's
Exchequer, have been from time to time
appropriated: thus we find in the reigns
of King William, Queen Anne, and Geo.
the First, the duties on coffee, malt, &c.
&c. appropriated to the payment of life-
annuities, annuities certain; and annuities arising from Lottery Tickets.   The
monies paid into the Exchequer, on account
of the subsidies of tonnage and bondage,
and of the several duties and rates payable on printed callicoes, and several other
merchandises, too tedious to mention,
were incorporated into one fund, called
the aggregate fund, (being a collection
of many particulars in one mass, or
body) but the monies arising from these
duties were never totally alienated, or
made chargeable with the payment of
as much money as the said duties a-
mounted to, because the civil list, which
is a revenue for the support and honor
of his Majesty's crown and dignity, in
the

the departments of his civil government,
arifes out of the faid duties : therefore if
at any time the monies paid into the Exchequer for thefe duties did not amount
to a furplus, above what they were
charged with for the payment of the intereft of money borrowed of the puplic ;
in that cafe the civil lift appointment
muft have fallen fhort, and the Exchequer have been indebted to the crown :
but when this has happened I cannot
take upon me to fay ; but as I apprehend, (and I hope I do not miftake, if
l do, I intreat the affiftance of fome abler
hand) there has often been a furplus or
excefs in time of peace, that is to fay,
after payment of the monies charged on
the faid aggregate fund, and the ap-
pointments of the civil lift, there has re-
mained monies in the Exchequer arifing
from the faid duties ; now thefe monies
have ever been at the difpofal of
parliament ; and I apprehend that thefe
furpluffes

furpluffes or exceffes, were made a new
fund, by the name of the finking fund,
about the year 1740; and ten years after this, when the act was paffed for the
reduction of intereft, in order to leffen
the national debt, we find the money
faved by the reduction of intereft is made
part of the finking fund; and the duties
(appropriated for the payment of the
intereft of feveral national debts) which
made part of the aggregate fund, are;
by this act, made part of the finking
fund; and for the future all furpluffes
and exceffes arifing in the Exchequer,
are made part of the finking fund, as
alfo all monies arifing from any taxes
levied for the payment of the intereft of
new contracted debts; and the payment
of the intereft of the money fo borrowed
is likewife charged upon the finking
fund; but for a fuller account of the
rife, progrefs, and prefent ftate of the
national debt, with the feveral revenues
appropriated to the payment of the fame;
and

and of the different methods ufed in raifing of money, and paying the intereſt
for it for many years paſt—I muſt refer
my readers to a large work, lately pub-
liſhed, intitled, The Merchant's Lawyer;
and ſhall conclude with confeſſing myfelf totally at a loſs to determine from
whence this fund took its name, unleſs
it be that it is chargeable with ſo many
debts, that it is impoſſible for it ever to
increaſe; but then there is one clauſe
in almoſt every act of parliament for
raiſing money, which ſeems to me to ſe-
cure it from diminiſhing; and therefore
I cannot apprehend, why it is called the
finking fund.   The clauſe is, that all
money that is iſſued out of the ſinking
fund, to make good any deficiences in
any of the duties appropriated for the
payment of the national debts charged
on this fund, ſhall be made good out of
the firſt aids granted by parliament.—
Upon the whole, what I have ſaid may
ſerve in ſome meaſure to gratify curioſity;
but

but the fubject appears not very important to the public in general, whofe
principal concern is, that the payment of
the intereft and the principal (in proper
time) of the money borrowed of them is
well fecured; and that it is, I hope no
Englifhmen will doubt, nor yet of the
enjoyment of every bleffing Heaven can
beftow, under the aufpicious government
of a moft amiable young monarch, bleffed
with every qualification for regal fway—
for whofe truly Britifh brow, the goddefs
of victory is preparing a crown of laurels,
to entwine with the regal diadem of the
realm

F I N I S.

A TABLE.

Exhibiting at one View, the intrinsic Value per Cent of the several Public Funds; and the proportion they bear to each other by which any person may know — which it will be most Advantageous to purchase, and what proportion such purchase bears, to the Value of Landed Estates; and Life Annuities.

3 per Cents at 60 are equal	to 3½ at 70	4 / 80	4½ / 90	5 / 100	5½ / 110	6 / 120	Years purchase 20	Annual Interest 5 per cent
61½	71¾	82	92¼	102½	112¾	123	20½	4 .. 17 .. 6
63	73½	84	94½	105	115½	126	21	4 .. 15 .. 2
64½	75¼	86	96¾	107½	118¼	129	21½	4 .. 13 .. -
66	77	88	99	110	121	132	22	4 .. 10 .. 10
67½	78¾	90	101¼	112½	123¾	135	22½	4 .. 8 .. 10
69	80½	92	103½	115	126½	138	23	4 .. 6 .. 11
70½	82¼	94	104¾	117½	129¼	141	23½	4 .. 5 .. 1
72	84	96	108	120	132	144	24	4 .. 3 .. 4

4.1.7	24½	147	134¾	122½	110¼	98	85¾	73½
4..--	25	150	137½	125	112½	100	87½	75
3.18.5	25½	153	140¼	127½	114¾	102	89¼	76½
3.16.11	26	156	143	130	117	104	91	78
3.15.5	26½	159	145¾	132½	119¼	106	92¾	79½
3.14.-	27	162	148½	135	121½	108	94½	81
3.12.8	27½	165	151¼	137½	123¾	110	96¼	82½
3.11.4	28	168	154	140	126	112	98	84
3.10.2	28½	171	156¾	142½	128¼	114	99¾	85½
3.9.-	29	174	159½	145	130½	116	101½	87
3.7.9	29½	177	162¼	147½	132¾	118	103¼	88½
3.6.8	30	180	165	150	135	120	105	90
3.5.7	30½	183	167¾	152½	137¼	122	106¾	91½
3.4.7	31	186	170½	155	139½	124	108½	93
3.3.5	31½	189	173¼	157½	141¾	126	110¼	94½

73½	85¾	98	110¼	122½	134¾	147	24½	4 . 1 . 7
75	87½	100	112½	125	137½	150	25	4 - " -
76½	89¼	102	114¾	127½	140¼	153	25½	3 . 18 . 5
78	91	104	117	130	143	156	26	3 . 16 . 11
79½	92¾	106	119¼	132½	145¾	159	26½	3 . 15 . 5
81	94½	108	121½	135	148½	162	27	3 . 14 -
82½	96¼	110	123¾	137½	151¼	165	27½	3 . 12 . 8
84	98	112	126	140	154	168	28	3 . 11 4
85½	99¾	114	128¼	142½	156¾	171	28½	3 . 10 . 2
87	101½	116	130½	145	159½	174	29	3 . 9 -
88½	103¼	118	132¾	147½	162¼	177	29½	3 . 7 . 9
90	105	120	135	150	165	180	30	3 . 6 . 8
91½	106¾	122	137¼	152½	167¾	183	30½	3 . 5 . 7
93	108½	124	139½	155	170½	186	31	3 . 4 . 7
94½	110¼	126	141¾	157½	173¼	189	31½	3 . 3 . 5

96	112	128	144	160	176	192	32	3 . 2 . 6
97½	113¾	130	146¼	162½	178¾	195	32½	3 . 1 . 6
99	115½	132	148½	165	181½	198	33	3 . 0 . 7
100½	117¼	134	150¾	167½	184¼	201	33½	2 . 19 . 8
102	119	136	153	170	187	204	34	2 . 18 . 10

Explanation of the above Table.

In the News Papers of this day July 27ᵗʰ 1761. Find what 3 per Cents —
Annuities, are at 82½, and India Stock at 141.

Query. Which of these will bring me in most Interest for Money, and what
Interest will each of them produce?

To know this, look in the first Column containing 3 per Cents for 82½, and
then in Column 9 by which you will find that 3 per Cents at 82½ produce £3. 12. 8ᵈ
per Annum. Then look in Column 7 for India Stock, and you will find 165.
which shews that when 3 per Cents are at 82½ India Stock is worth 165. in value proportion,
bringing in the same Annual Interest of 3ˡ. 12. 8ᵈ. so that by the price in the papers
Viz:ᵗ 141. it appears that s India Stock is 24 per Cent Cheaper than 3 per Cents at 82 2/10ᵗ this Rule
so obviously gives the just value of all the intermediate Funds that it requires no further explanation.

NB: After having made a just Estimate of the value of each of the Funds you are at liberty
if you think proper to refer to the remarks contained in, Every man his own Broker!
concerning the differences of the several Securities.

Printed for S. Hooper at Cæsar's Head Strand. Price 6ᵈ.

Printed in the United States
By Bookmasters